Health-Care CareerVision ™

Book and DVD

View What You'd Do

The Editors @ JIST

JIST Works
America's Career Publisher

Health-Care CareerVision Book and DVD
View What You'd Do

© 2008 by JIST Publishing

Published by JIST Works, an imprint of JIST Publishing
7321 Shadeland Station, Suite 200
Indianapolis, IN 46256-3923

Phone: 800-648-JIST   Fax: 877-454-7839
E-mail: info@jist.com   Web site: www.jist.com

Quantity discounts are available for JIST products. Have future editions of JIST books automatically delivered to you on publication through our convenient standing order program. Please call our Sales Department at 800-648-JIST for a free catalog and more information.

Visit www.jist.com for information on JIST, free job search tips, book excerpts, and online ordering.

Acquisitions Editor: Susan Pines
Writer and Database Work: Laurence Shatkin, Ph.D.
Development Editor: Heather Stith
Cover Designer: Trudy Coler
Cover Photographers: Glowimages/Getty Images; Duncan Smith/Photodisc Green/Getty Images; Laurent Hamels/PhotoAlto/Getty Images
Interior Designer and Layout: Marie Kristine Parial-Leonardo
Proofreaders: Linda Siefert, Jeanne Clark
Indexer: Kelly D. Henthorne

Printed in United States of America

12 11 10 09 08 07   9 8 7 6 5 4 3 2 1

Library of Congress Cataloging-in-Publication Data

Health-care careervision book and DVD : view what you'd do / the editors at JIST.
    p. cm.
Includes index.
  ISBN 978-1-59357-463-5 (includes dvd : alk. paper)
 1. Allied health personnel—Vocational guidance. 2. Medical personnel—Vocational guidance. I. JIST Works, Inc.
  R697.A4.H3815 2008
  610.73'7023—dc22

2007024681

ISBN 978-1-59357-463-5

Open Your Eyes to America's Hottest Career Field

More than 13 million people are working in the health-care field. Are you thinking about joining them? This field is growing so fast that it is full of opportunities for rewarding work. With this book and the accompanying DVD, you can see what 72 health-care jobs are like: the work tasks, the pay, the job outlook, the work settings, and lots of other useful insights.

You don't need to go to medical school to get a good health-care job. In fact, almost one-quarter of the jobs included in this book require only on-the-job training. More than half require less than a bachelor's degree. The job descriptions in the book are organized by level of education or training required, so you can easily find jobs with a level of preparation that is right for you.

If you're not sure what health-care jobs might suit you, you can complete a checklist based on personality types to clarify your preferences. Or you can browse lists of health-care jobs organized to highlight those with the best pay, the fastest growth, and the most job openings. If you think best visually, you can browse the videos on the DVD until you find some that interest you, and then open the book to learn the details about the jobs. Using this book and DVD, you'll be surprised how quickly you'll get new ideas for career goals in this dynamic field.

Health-Care CareerVision at a Glance

This book is divided into four chapters:

➤ Chapter 1, "Health Care: The Big Picture," provides an overview of the health-care field. It covers such important topics as the major sectors of the field, the working conditions, the size and characteristics of the workforce, the major occupations in the field, how people prepare for the field and advance in it, job opportunities in the field, earnings, and sources of additional information.

➤ Chapter 2, "Which Health-Care Jobs Are Right for You?" provides a checklist to help you decide which health-care jobs are the best matches for your personality. The checklist takes only a few minutes to complete and is based on the personality theory developed by John Holland.

➤ Chapter 3, "Spotlight on the Best Health-Care Jobs," is very useful for exploring health-care career options. The lists in this chapter present the best health-care jobs according to various criteria: the best jobs overall (based on their combined rankings on earnings, job growth, and job openings), the best-paying jobs, the fastest-growing jobs, and the jobs with the most openings.

➤ Chapter 4, "Health-Care Careers in Focus," provides complete descriptions of the 72 jobs that appear on the lists in Chapter 3. Each description has a corresponding video on the DVD and contains information on work tasks, skills, earnings, projected growth, work environment, and many other details.

This book also includes five appendixes to explain how to use the DVD, where we got the information for this book, what the skills listed in the job descriptions mean, how the interest area structure is organized, and where to find more information related to this topic.

Table of Contents

Chapter 4: Health-Care Careers in Focus   41

Appendix A: Technical Help in Using the DVD   195

Appendix B: Background on the Career Information Used in This Book   197

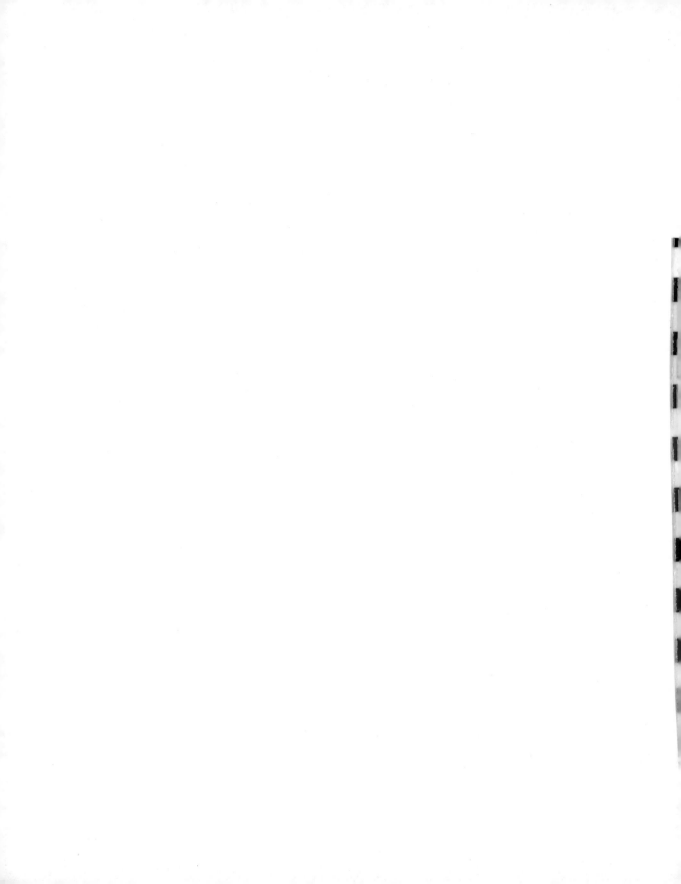

Introduction

If a picture is worth a thousand words, then this book and the DVD that comes with it are equivalent to an encyclopedia. Together, they provide the most important facts about 72 health-care careers and also show real workers and work settings.

How This Resource Can Help You

With the information in this book and DVD, you can

➤ Develop career plans for a job in the health-care field.

➤ Decide on an education or training program that will prepare you for a good job in health care.

➤ Identify health-care jobs that can make use of experience and skills you already have.

➤ Prepare for interviews by learning how to connect your skills to your career goal.

How to Best Use This Resource

You may want to start by immediately popping the DVD into your computer's DVD player or by browsing the book, but keep in mind that this resource is organized to help you through a process of career exploration. The organization is flexible; it's designed to be used by different people in different ways.

Read over the following list to see where you fit in:

➤ **I want to choose a career, but I don't have a clear idea which job might be best for me.** To decide whether the health-care field is a good choice for you, read Chapter 1 and view Video 1 for an overview of this fast-growing industry. Then find a pencil and sit down with Chapter 2 to complete a checklist that will help you think about what types of work best suit your personality. A table at the end of the chapter shows you job titles in the health-care field associated with each personality type. Next, look up intriguing jobs in Chapter 4 and read the detailed job descriptions. Each description identifies the video number so that you can find the related video on the DVD. Another strategy is to pop the DVD into your computer's DVD player and view one video after another, jotting down the titles of jobs that seem particularly interesting. Then you can look them up in Chapter 4 for a more in-depth understanding. A different approach is to look over the lists in Chapter 3 (for example, the list of the best-paying health-care jobs), find job titles that grab your attention, and look them up in Chapter 4 and on the DVD.

➤ **I have a health-care career in mind, but I'm not yet certain about it.** You will be able to make a more informed decision after you read the description of the job in Chapter 4 and view its related video on the DVD. Each job description includes a section on "Where to Find Out More," and Appendix E suggests more resources where you can continue to research your tentative career choice. If what you learn makes you *less* committed to your current career goal, you may consider related jobs. The table at the end of Chapter 2 lists jobs that are linked to the same personality type. Or you may want to get fresh ideas by browsing the "best" health-care jobs lists in Chapter 3, the job descriptions in Chapter 4, or the videos on the DVD.

➤ **I'm a midlife career changer.** If you are looking for jobs that do not require a lot of additional education or training, you will be pleased to note that the 72 jobs described in Chapter 4 are arranged by the amount of education or training they require. Those that require the shortest course of education or training are closest to the beginning of the chapter. Each description also notes whether certification or licensure is required. When you read the job descriptions in Chapter 4 and view the related videos, pay attention to the skills identified there and make note of jobs that use skills you have developed through your work and leisure-time experiences. You may also look for work settings where you have experience or a high level of comfort.

We hope you find this book as interesting to browse as we did to put together. We have tried to make it easy to use and as interesting as occupational information can be. When you have finished using this book, pass it along or tell someone else about it. We wish you well in your career and in your life.

Credits and Acknowledgments: Although the authors created this book, it is based on the work of many others. The occupational information is based on data obtained from the U.S. Department of Labor and the U.S. Census Bureau. These sources provide the most authoritative occupational information available. The job titles and their related descriptions are from the O*NET database, which was developed by researchers and developers under the direction of the U.S. Department of Labor. They, in turn, were assisted by thousands of employers who provided details on the nature of work in the many thousands of job samplings used in the database's development. We used the most recent version of the O*NET database, release 11.0. We appreciate and thank the staff of the U.S. Department of Labor for their efforts and expertise in providing such a rich source of data. The career videos were developed and distributed by the New Jersey Center for Occupational Employment Information under a grant from the U.S. Department of Labor, Employment and Training Administration. They are designed to provide a brief, visual introduction to careers and the world of work.

CHAPTER 1

Health Care: The Big Picture

video number

Combining medical technology and the human touch, health-care workers administer care around the clock, responding to the needs of millions of people—from newborns to the critically ill. Not only is health care an important field, but it is also the nation's largest, employing more than 13 million people. This chapter gives an overview of the health-care field so that you'll understand the available opportunities. In addition to reading this chapter, you also should view Video 1 on the DVD.

Changes in Health Care

In the rapidly changing health-care field, technological advances have made possible many new procedures and methods of diagnosis and treatment. Clinical developments, such as organ transplants, less-invasive surgical techniques, skin grafts, and gene therapy for cancer treatment, continue to increase the longevity and improve the quality of life of many Americans. Advances in medical technology also have improved the survival rates of people who are severely ill or are victims of trauma. These people need extensive care from therapists and social workers as well as other support personnel.

In addition, advances in information technology continue to improve patient care and worker efficiency. For example, handheld computers are used to record notes on each patient, and then information on vital signs and orders for tests are transferred electronically to a main database. This process eliminates the need for paper and reduces record-keeping errors.

Cost containment also is shaping the health-care field, as shown by the growing emphasis on providing services on an outpatient, ambulatory basis; limiting unnecessary or low-priority services; and stressing preventive care, which reduces the potential cost of undiagnosed, untreated medical conditions. Enrollment in managed care programs—predominantly preferred provider organizations, health maintenance organizations, and hybrid plans such as point-of-service programs—continues to grow. These prepaid plans provide comprehensive coverage to members and control health insurance costs by emphasizing preventive care. Cost-effectiveness also is improved with the increased use of integrated delivery systems, which combine two or more types of health-care establishments in order to increase efficiency through the streamlining of functions, primarily financial and managerial. These changes will continue to reshape not only the nature of the health-care workforce, but also the manner in which health care is provided.

Types of Workplaces

An establishment is a place where people work. The health-care field consists of about 545,000 establishments. Although these establishments vary greatly in terms of size, staffing patterns, and organizational structures, they each fit into one of the following nine types:

➤ **Home health-care services:** Skilled nursing or medical care is sometimes provided in the home under a physician's supervision. Home health-care services are provided mainly to the elderly. The development of in-home medical technologies, substantial cost savings, and patients' preference for home care have helped change this once-small part of the health-care field into one of the fastest-growing parts of the economy.

➤ **Hospitals:** Hospitals provide complete medical care, ranging from diagnostic services to surgery to continuous nursing care. Some hospitals specialize in treatment of people who are mentally ill, cancer patients, or children. Hospital-based care may be on an inpatient (overnight) or outpatient basis. The mix of workers needed varies, depending on the size, geographic location, goals, philosophy, funding, organization, and management style of the institution. As hospitals work to improve efficiency, care continues to shift from an inpatient to outpatient basis whenever possible. Many hospitals have expanded into long-term and home health-care services, providing a wide range of care for the communities they serve.

➤ **Medical and diagnostic laboratories:** This type of establishment provides analytic or diagnostic services to the medical profession or directly to patients following a physician's prescription. Workers may analyze blood, take X-rays and computerized tomography scans, or perform other clinical tests. Medical and diagnostic laboratories provide the fewest number of jobs in the health-care field.

➤ **Nursing and residential care facilities:** Nursing care facilities provide inpatient nursing, rehabilitation, and health-related personal care to those who need continuous nursing care but do not require hospital services. Nursing aides provide the vast majority of direct care. Other facilities, such as convalescent homes, help patients who need less assistance.

In residential care facilities, nursing and medical care are not the main functions. Workers in these facilities instead focus on providing around-the-clock social and personal care to children, the elderly, and others who have limited ability to care for themselves. Residential care facilities include assisted-living facilities, alcohol and drug rehabilitation centers, group homes, and halfway houses.

➤ **Offices of dentists:** About one out of every five health-care establishments is a dentist's office. Most employ only a few workers, who provide general or specialized dental care, including dental surgery.

➤ **Offices of physicians:** About 37 percent of all health-care establishments fit this description. Physicians and surgeons practice privately or in groups of practitioners who have the same or different specialties. Many physicians and surgeons prefer to join group practices because they provide backup coverage, reduce overhead expenses, and facilitate consultation with peers. Physicians and surgeons are increasingly working as salaried employees of group medical practices, clinics, or integrated health systems.

➤ **Offices of other health practitioners:** This type of establishment includes the offices of chiropractors, optometrists, podiatrists, occupational and physical therapists, psychologists, audiologists, speech-language pathologists, dietitians, and other health practitioners. Demand for these services is related to the ability of patients to pay, either directly or through health insurance. Hospitals and nursing care facilities may contract out for these services. This group also includes the offices of practitioners of alternative medicine, such as acupuncturists, homeopaths, hypnotherapists, and naturopaths.

➤ **Outpatient care centers:** The diverse establishments in this group include kidney dialysis centers, outpatient mental health and substance abuse centers, health maintenance organization medical centers, and freestanding ambulatory surgical and emergency centers.

➤ **Other ambulatory health-care services:** This relatively small group includes ambulance and helicopter transport services, blood and organ banks, and other ambulatory health-care services, such as pacemaker monitoring services and smoking cessation programs.

The following table breaks down the health-care field in terms of the percent of the total number of health-care establishments that fit into each type (Establishments) and the percent of the total number of health-care workers that are employed in each type of establishment (Employment). (These numbers are taken from the most recent year for which data is available, 2004.) Note that about 76 percent of health-care establishments are offices of physicians, dentists, or other health practitioners. Although hospitals constitute only 2 percent of all health-care establishments, they employ 40 percent of all health-care workers.

PERCENT DISTRIBUTION OF TYPES OF HEALTH-CARE ESTABLISHMENTS AND NUMBER OF HEALTH-CARE JOBS

Establishment Type	Establishments	Employment
Home health-care services	3.0%	5.8%
Hospitals, public and private	1.9%	41.3%
Medical and diagnostic laboratories	2.1%	1.4%
Nursing and residential care facilities	11.6%	21.3%
Offices of dentists	21.0%	5.7%
Offices of physicians	37.0%	15.5%
Offices of other health practitioners	18.7%	4.0%
Outpatient care centers	3.2%	3.4%
Other ambulatory health-care services	1.5%	1.5%

The size of the establishment affects a job's characteristics. A larger establishment may provide a greater range of positions and more opportunities for advancement. A job in a smaller establishment may offer a greater variety of duties and thus provide a broader range of experience.

The health-care field includes establishments ranging from small-town private practices of physicians who employ only one medical assistant to busy inner-city hospitals that have thousands of diverse jobs. The following charts illustrate how many workers nonhospital health-care establishments and hospitals are likely to employ. For the most part, hospitals tend to be large establishments that employ hundreds of health-care workers at each location, but other types of health-care establishments tend to be small, with the majority employing fewer than 20 employees.

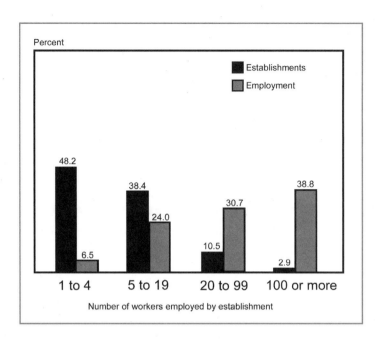

Percent

■ Establishments
▨ Employment

48.2
6.5
38.4
24.0
10.5
30.7
2.9
38.8

1 to 4   5 to 19   20 to 99   100 or more

Number of workers employed by establishment

This chart shows the percentage of nonhospital health services establishments that employ certain numbers of health care workers (as of March 2004). Note that about half of these establishments employed fewer than five workers.

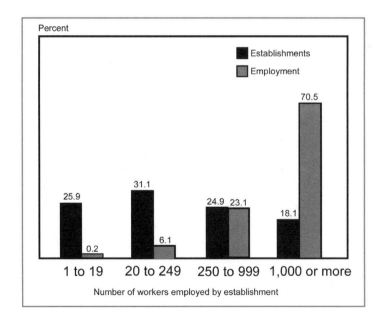

Percent

■ Establishments
▨ Employment

70.5
25.9
0.2
31.1
6.1
24.9 23.1
18.1

1 to 19   20 to 249   250 to 999   1,000 or more

Number of workers employed by establishment

This chart shows the percentage of hospitals that employ certain numbers of health care workers (as of March 2004). Note that 7 out of 10 hospital employees worked in establishments with more than 1,000 employees.

Working Conditions

Average weekly hours of nonsupervisory workers in private health care vary among the different types of establishments. Many health-care establishments operate around the clock and need staff at all hours. Shift work is common in some occupations, such as registered nurses. According to the most recent data, workers in dentists' offices averaged only 26.9 hours per week, and those in psychiatric and substance abuse hospitals averaged 36.4 hours, compared with 33.7 hours for all nongovernment fields. Numerous health-care workers hold more than one job.

Many workers in the health-care field are on part-time schedules. Students, parents with young children, dual jobholders, and older workers make up much of the part-time workforce. Part-time workers made up about 20 percent of the workforce as a whole in 2004, but they accounted for 39 percent of workers in dentists' offices and 33 percent of those in offices of other health practitioners.

A career in health care involves some physical risks. Health-care workers involved in direct patient care must take precautions to prevent back strain from lifting patients and equipment; to minimize exposure to radiation and caustic chemicals; and to guard against infectious diseases, such as AIDS, tuberculosis, and hepatitis. Home care personnel are exposed to the possibility of overexerting themselves when assisting patients, falling inside or outside of patients' homes, and being injured in highway accidents while traveling to and from homes. In 2004, the incidence of occupational injury and illness in hospitals was 8.7 cases per 100 full-time workers, compared with an average of 5 cases for nongovernment fields overall. Nursing care facilities had a much higher rate of 10.1.

Employment

The most recent data collected about the health-care field revealed some interesting facts:

➤ Health-care jobs are found throughout the country, but they are concentrated in the most populous states: California, New York, Florida, Texas, and Pennsylvania.

➤ About 92 percent of wage and salary jobs were in nongovernment establishments. The rest were in state and local government hospitals.

➤ The health-care field includes about 411,000 jobs for self-employed and unpaid family workers. The majority of these jobs (about 282,000) were in offices of physicians, dentists, and other health practitioners.

➤ Workers in health care tend to be older than workers in other fields.

➤ Health-care workers also are more likely than workers in other fields to remain employed in the same occupation, due in part to the high level of education and training required for many health-care occupations.

Types of Occupations

Health-care firms employ large numbers of workers in professional and service occupations. Together, these occupational groups account for three out of four jobs in the field. The next largest share of jobs, 18 percent, is in office and administrative support. Management, business, and financial operations occupations account for only 4 percent of employment. Other occupations in health care make up only 3 percent of the total. The following table breaks down the health-care field into occupational groups and occupations and shows the latest data concerning the number of jobs in each of these groups and occupations and by what percentage that number is projected to grow in the coming years (the decade ending in 2014).

EMPLOYMENT OF WAGE AND SALARY WORKERS IN HEALTH CARE BY OCCUPATION AND PROJECTED GROWTH

Occupation	Number of Jobs	Percentage of Field	Projected Growth
Total, all occupations	13,062,000	100.0%	27.3%
Management, business, and financial occupations	574,000	4.4%	28.3%
Medical and health services managers	175,000	1.3%	26.1%
Top executives	101,000	0.8%	33.3%
Office and administrative support occupations	2,379,000	18.2%	16.2%
Billing and posting clerks and machine operators	179,000	1.4%	10.9%
Medical secretaries	347,000	2.7%	17.3%
Receptionists and information clerks	353,000	2.7%	31.3%
Professional and related occupations	5,657,000	43.3%	27.8%
Chiropractors	21,000	0.2%	47.8%
Clinical laboratory technologists and technicians	257,000	2.0%	22.7%
Counselors	152,000	1.2%	31.8%
Dental hygienists	153,000	1.2%	43.7%
Dentists	95,000	0.7%	18.5%

(continued)

(continued)

EMPLOYMENT OF WAGE AND SALARY WORKERS IN HEALTH CARE BY OCCUPATION AND PROJECTED GROWTH

Occupation	Number of Jobs	Percentage of Field	Projected Growth
Diagnostic-related technologists and technicians	269,000	2.1%	26.4%
Dietitians and nutritionists	32,000	0.2%	20.1%
Emergency medical technicians and paramedics	122,000	0.9%	27.8%
Health diagnosing and treating practitioner support technicians	226,000	1.7%	18.0%
Health educators	17,000	0.1%	27.0%
Licensed practical and licensed vocational nurses	586,000	4.5%	14.2%
Medical records and health information technicians	134,000	1.0%	30.0%
Optometrists	18,000	0.1%	29.6%
Pharmacists	63,000	0.5%	17.3%
Physicians and surgeons	417,000	3.2%	28.7%
Physician assistants	53,000	0.4%	54.8%
Podiatrists	7,000	0.1%	22.2%
Psychologists	33,000	0.3%	28.1%
Registered nurses	1,988,000	15.2%	30.5%
Social workers	169,000	1.3%	29.3%
Social and human service assistants	99,000	0.8%	38.6%
Therapists (occupational, physical, radiation, etc.)	358,000	2.7%	32.8%
Service occupations	4,152,000	31.8%	33.2%
Building cleaning workers	365,000	2.8%	20.6%
Dental assistants	257,000	2.0%	43.6%
Food preparation and serving-related occupations	462,000	3.5%	12.6%

Occupation	Number of Jobs	Percentage of Field	Projected Growth
Home health aides	458,000	3.5%	66.4%
Medical assistants	361,000	2.8%	53.7%
Medical transcriptionists	81,000	0.6%	22.1%
Nursing aides, orderlies, and attendants	1,230,000	9.4%	22.2%
Physical therapist assistants and aides	95,000	0.7%	41.0%
Personal and home care aides	312,000	2.4%	60.5%

Note: The specific numbers for the occupations may not add to totals given for the occupational group due to the omission of occupations with small employment.

Professional occupations, such as dentists, registered nurses, and social workers, usually require at least a bachelor's degree in a specialized field or higher education in a specific health field (although registered nurses also can enter the occupation through associate degree or diploma programs). Professional workers often have high levels of responsibility and complex duties. In addition to providing services, these workers may supervise other workers or conduct research.

The professional occupational group also includes technicians and other health professionals in fast-growing occupations such as medical records and health information technicians and dental hygienists. These workers may operate technical equipment and assist practitioners who diagnose and treat health conditions. These jobs usually require specific formal training beyond high school, but less than four years of college. Many workers in these types of jobs are graduates of one- or two-year training programs.

Service occupations, such as nursing aides, dental assistants, and personal and home care aides, attract many workers with little or no specialized education or training. Although some of these workers are employed by public or private agencies, many are self-employed. With experience and, in some cases, further education and training, service workers may advance to higher-level positions or transfer to new occupations.

Although most health-care workers provide clinical services, many also are employed in occupations with other functions. For example, office and administrative support occupations in health care include medical secretaries and receptionists and information clerks. These workers may be trained on the job or may need postsecondary vocational training. Other health-care workers are employed in management, business, and financial occupations. These workers usually have an associate or higher degree. Although many medical and health services managers have a background in a clinical specialty or training in health-care administration, some enter these jobs with a general business education, usually a bachelor's degree. All of these workers keep health-care organizations running smoothly.

Each type of health-care establishment provides a different mix of wage and salary health-care jobs:

➤ **Home health-care services:** About 57 percent of all jobs in these establishments are in service occupations, mostly home health aides and personal and home care aides. Nursing and therapist jobs also account for substantial shares of employment in this type of establishment.

➤ **Hospitals:** Hospitals employ workers with all levels of education and training, thereby providing a wider variety of services than is offered by other segments of the health-care field. About 3 in 10 hospital workers are registered nurses. Hospitals also employ many physicians and surgeons, therapists, and social workers. About 1 in 5 hospital jobs are in a service occupation, such as nursing aides or building cleaning workers. Hospitals also employ large numbers of office and administrative support workers.

➤ **Medical and diagnostic laboratories:** Professional and related workers, primarily clinical laboratory technologists and technicians, make up about 43 percent of all jobs in these establishments. Service workers employed in these establishments include medical assistants and medical transcriptionists.

➤ **Nursing and residential care facilities:** About two out of three nursing and residential care facility jobs are in service occupations, primarily nursing and home health aides. Professional and administrative support occupations make up a much smaller percentage of employment in these establishments compared to other parts of the health-care field. Federal law requires nursing facilities to have licensed personnel on hand 24 hours a day and to maintain an appropriate level of care.

➤ **Offices of dentists:** Roughly one-third of all jobs in these establishments are in service occupations, mostly dental assistants. The typical staffing pattern in dentists' offices consists of one dentist with a support staff of dental hygienists and dental assistants. Larger practices are more likely to employ office managers and administrative support workers.

➤ **Offices of physicians:** Many of the jobs in offices of physicians are in professional and related occupations, primarily physicians, surgeons, and registered nurses. About two-fifths of all jobs, however, are in office and administrative support occupations, such as receptionists and information clerks.

➤ **Offices of other health practitioners:** Professional occupations, such as chiropractors, accounted for about two out of five jobs in these establishments. Related occupations, such as medical records technicians and nurses, also accounted for a significant portion of jobs, as did office and administrative support occupations.

➤ **Outpatient care centers:** These establishments employ a high percentage of professional and related workers, including counselors, social workers, and registered nurses.

➤ **Other ambulatory health-care services:** Because this group includes ambulance services, it employs two out of every five emergency medical technicians and paramedics.

Training and Advancement

Maybe you're worried about whether you can handle the years of college preparation you'll need for a career in health care. The good news is that most health-care workers have jobs that require less than four years of education.

A variety of programs after high school provide specialized training for jobs in health care. Students preparing for health careers can enter programs leading to a certificate or a degree at the associate, baccalaureate, or graduate level. Two-year programs resulting in certificates or associate degrees are the minimum standard credential for occupations such as dental hygienist or radiologic technologist. Most therapists and social workers have at least a bachelor's degree. Health diagnosing and treating practitioners—such as physicians and surgeons, optometrists, and podiatrists—are among the most educated workers, with many years of education and training beyond college.

The health-care field also provides many job opportunities for people without specialized training beyond high school. In fact, more than half of workers in nursing and residential care facilities have a high school diploma or less, as do a quarter of workers in hospitals.

Some health-care establishments provide on-the-job or classroom training as well as continuing education. For example, in all certified nursing facilities, nursing aides must complete a state-approved training and competency evaluation program and participate in at least 12 hours of in-service education annually. Hospitals are more likely than other facilities to have the resources and incentive to provide training programs and advancement opportunities to their employees. In other segments of health care, the variety of positions and advancement opportunities are more limited. Larger establishments usually offer a broader range of opportunities.

Some hospitals provide training or tuition assistance in return for a promise to work at their facility for a particular length of time after graduation. Many nursing facilities have similar programs. Some hospitals have cross-training programs that train their workers—through formal college programs, continuing education, or in-house training—to perform functions outside their specialties.

Health specialists with clinical expertise can advance to department head positions or even higher-level management jobs. Medical and health services managers can advance to more responsible positions all the way up to chief executive officer.

Outlook

Job opportunities should be excellent in all health-care employment settings in the years to come. Consider these facts:

➤ The health care field is expected to swell by more than 27 percent by 2014, compared with 14 percent for all other fields combined.

➤ Of the 20 occupations expected to grow the fastest in the next several years, 8 are in health care. For example, total employment of home health aides—including the self-employed—is projected to increase by 56 percent, medical assistants by 52 percent, physician assistants by 50 percent, and physical therapist assistants by 44 percent.

➤ By 2014, 3.6 million new wage and salary jobs (in contrast to jobs done by self-employed or unpaid workers) will be created in health care. This number is about 19 percent of all new jobs, more than in any other field.

➤ Tougher immigration rules are slowing the numbers of foreign health-care workers entering the United States.

➤ Many health-care workers, who tend to be older than workers in other fields, are expected to retire during the next several years.

Employment in health care will continue to grow for several reasons. The number of people in older age groups with much greater than average health-care needs is growing faster than the total population. As a result, the demand for health care will increase. Employment in home health care and nursing and residential care should increase rapidly as life expectancies rise and as aging children are less able to care for their parents and rely more on long-term care facilities. Advances in medical technology will continue to improve the survival rate of severely ill and injured patients, who will then need extensive therapy and care. New technologies will make it possible to identify and treat conditions that were previously not treatable. Medical group practices and integrated health systems will become larger and more complex, increasing the need for office and administrative support workers.

Many job openings will result from a need to replace workers due to retirements and high job turnover. Occupations with the most replacement openings are usually large, with high turnover stemming from low pay and status, poor benefits, low training requirements, and a high proportion of young and part-time workers. Nursing aides, orderlies, and attendants, and home health aides are among the occupations adding the most new jobs by 2014, about 675,000 combined. In contrast, occupations with relatively few replacement openings, such as physicians and surgeons, are characterized by high pay and status, lengthy training requirements, and a high proportion of full-time workers.

Another occupation that will add many new jobs is registered nurses. The median age of registered nurses is increasing, and not enough younger workers are replacing them. As a result, employers in some parts of the country are reporting difficulties in attracting and retaining nurses. Imbalances between the supply of and the demand for qualified workers should spur efforts to attract and retain qualified registered nurses. For example, employers may restructure workloads and job responsibilities, improve compensation and working conditions, and subsidize training or continuing education.

Demand for dental care will rise due to population growth, greater retention of natural teeth by middle-aged and older persons, greater awareness of the importance of dental care, and an increased ability to pay for services. Dentists will use support personnel such as dental hygienists and assistants to help meet their increased workloads.

In some management, business, and financial operations occupations, rapid growth will be tempered by restructuring to reduce administrative costs and streamline operations. Many facilities will cut the number of middle managers while simultaneously creating new managerial positions as the facilities diversify. Office automation and other technological changes will slow employment growth in office and administrative support occupations, but because the employment base is large, replacement needs will continue to create substantial numbers of job openings. Slower-growing service occupations also will provide job openings due to replacement needs.

The shift from inpatient to less-expensive outpatient and home health care (because of improvements in diagnostic tests and surgical procedures along with patients' desires to be treated at home) is likely to result in fast growth in occupations concentrated outside the inpatient hospital sector, such as medical assistants and home health aides. Because of cost pressures, many health-care facilities will adjust their staffing patterns to reduce labor costs. Where patient care demands and regulations allow, health-care facilities will substitute lower-paid providers and will cross-train their workforces.

Traditional inpatient hospital positions will no longer be the only option for many health-care workers. Employment growth in hospitals will be the slowest within the health-care field because of efforts to control hospital costs and the increasing use of outpatient clinics and other alternative care sites. Persons seeking a career in health care will have to be willing to work in various employment settings.

The following table shows the current (as of 2004) employment for each type of health-care establishment and the projected rates of employment growth (between 2004 and 2014) for each type. These rates range from 13 percent in hospitals, the largest and slowest-growing establishments, to 69 percent in the much smaller home health-care services.

EMPLOYMENT AND PROJECTED CHANGE IN HEALTH-CARE ESTABLISHMENTS

Type of Establishment	Employment	Percent Change
Home health-care services	773,000	69.5%
Hospitals, public and private	5,301,000	13.1%
Medical and diagnostic laboratories	189,000	27.1%
Nursing and residential care facilities	2,815,000	27.8%
Offices of dentists	760,000	31.7%
Offices of physicians	2,054,000	37.0%
Offices of other health practitioners	524,000	42.7%
Outpatient care centers	446,000	44.2%
Other ambulatory health-care services	201,000	37.7%

Health-care workers at all levels of education and training will continue to be in demand. In many cases, job seekers with health-specific training will be able to obtain jobs and advance in their careers more easily than those workers without such training. Specialized clinical training is a requirement for many jobs in health care and is an asset even for many administrative jobs that do not specifically require it.

Earnings

Earnings in individual health-care occupations vary depending on the duties, level of education and training, and amount of responsibility required by the occupation. As in most fields, professionals and managers working in health care typically earn more than other workers in the field.

Average earnings of nonsupervisory workers in most health-care establishments are higher than the average for all nongovernment fields, with hospital workers earning considerably more than the average and those employed in nursing and residential care facilities and home health-care services earning less. Average earnings often are higher in hospitals because the percentage of jobs requiring higher levels of education and training is greater than in other establishments. In contrast, nursing and residential care facilities and home health-care services employ large numbers of part-time service workers. The first table shows the latest available data (2004) about average hours and earnings in each of the different types of establishments in the health-care field. The second table shows how earnings for the same job can vary by type of establishment.

AVERAGE EARNINGS AND HOURS OF NONSUPERVISORY WORKERS IN HEALTH CARE BY TYPE OF ESTABLISHMENT

Establishment	Weekly Earnings	Hourly Earnings	Weekly Hours
Total, nongovernment	$528.56	$15.67	33.7
Health care	$572.83	$17.32	33.1
Home health-care services	$415.12	$14.41	28.8
Hospitals	$715.12	$20.31	35.2
Medical and diagnostic laboratories	$634.79	$18.15	35.0
Nursing and residential care facilities	$393.58	$12.05	32.7
Offices of dentists	$510.81	$18.96	26.9
Offices of physicians	$613.82	$18.41	33.4
Offices of other health practitioners	$453.91	$16.00	28.4
Outpatient care centers	$631.38	$18.57	34.0
Other ambulatory health-care services	$498.65	$14.32	34.8

MEDIAN HOURLY EARNINGS OF THE LARGEST OCCUPATIONS IN HEALTH CARE

Occupation	Ambulatory Health-Care Services	Hospitals	Nursing and Residential Care Facilities	All Fields
Dental assistants	$13.60	$14.02	No data	$13.62
Home health aides	$8.58	$9.69	$8.84	$8.81
Licensed practical and licensed vocational nurses	$15.59	$15.71	$16.95	$16.33
Medical assistants	$11.77	$12.03	$10.85	$11.83
Medical secretaries	$12.88	$12.60	$12.00	$12.76
Nursing aides, orderlies, and attendants	$9.82	$10.43	$9.78	$10.09

(continued)

(continued)

MEDIAN HOURLY EARNINGS OF THE LARGEST OCCUPATIONS IN HEALTH CARE

Occupation	Ambulatory Health-Care Services	Hospitals	Nursing and Residential Care Facilities	All Fields
Office clerks	$11.07	$11.08	$9.62	$10.50
Personal and home care aides	$7.05	$8.54	$8.85	$8.12
Receptionists and information clerks	$10.76	$11.79	$10.40	$10.95
Registered nurses	$23.69	$25.66	$22.93	$25.16

Earnings vary not only by type of establishment, but also by size. Salaries tend to be higher in larger hospitals and group practices. Some establishments also offer tuition reimbursement, paid training, child day care services, and flexible work hours. Health-care establishments that must be staffed around the clock to care for patients and handle emergencies often pay premiums for overtime and weekend work, holidays, late shifts, and time spent on call. Bonuses and profit-sharing payments also may add to earnings. Geographic location also can affect earnings.

Although some hospitals have unions, the health-care field is not heavily unionized. In 2004, only 11 percent of workers in the field were members of unions or covered by union contracts, compared with about 14 percent for all fields.

Sources of Additional Information

General information on health careers is available from

➤ Bureau of Health Professions, Parklawn Rm. 8A-09, 5600 Fishers Lane, Rockville, MD 20857. Internet: bhpr.hrsa.gov/kidscareers

For a list of accredited programs in allied health fields, contact

➤ Commission on Accreditation of Allied Health Education Programs, 1361 Park Street, Clearwater, FL 33756. Internet: www.caahep.org

For information about specific careers in the health-care field, turn to Chapter 3 and Chapter 4 of this book and the DVD that accompanies it. Appendix E lists more resources you can turn to for further career exploration.

CHAPTER 2

Which Health-Care Jobs Are Right for You?

Anyone considering a career in health care should have a strong desire to help others, genuine concern for the welfare of patients and clients, and an ability to deal with people of diverse backgrounds in stressful situations. If you have these basic traits, it's time to consider exactly which health-care jobs are right for you. In the following pages, you're going to gain some insights into the work-related aspects of your personality and learn which of the 72 health-care careers in this book best suit your personality. Of course, personality is not the only factor you should consider when you make a career choice, but it's a good place to start because it provides a big-picture view of the world of work.

The Holland Personality Types

The most widely used personality theory about careers was developed by John L. Holland in the early 1950s. The theory rests on the principle that people tend to be happier and more successful in jobs where they feel comfortable with the work tasks and problems, the physical environment, and the kinds of people who are coworkers. Holland identified six personality types that describe basic aspects of work situations. He called them Realistic, Investigative, Artistic, Social, Enterprising, and Conventional. (Some of these labels are difficult to grasp at first glance, but you'll gain a clearer understanding by the time you finish this chapter.) The combination of initials for these personality types, RIASEC, is often used to refer to these six types.

Holland argued that most people can be described by one of the RIASEC personality types—the type that dominates—and that likewise each of the various occupations that make up the U.S. economy can be described as having work situations and settings compatible with one of these personality types. Therefore, if you understand your dominant personality type and then identify which jobs are consistent with that type, you will have a clearer idea of which jobs will suit you best. No matter what your dominant personality type is, you can find careers in the health-care field that are worth considering.

Holland recognized that many people and jobs also tend toward a second or third personality type. For example, someone might be described primarily as Social and secondarily as Investigative, and such a person would fit in best working in a job with the *SI* code, such as registered nurses. People matching this description should also consider jobs coded *IS,* such as physician assistants, and they might find satisfaction in many jobs with a variety of three-letter Holland codes beginning with either S or I.

The next section provides a checklist to help you clarify your main RIASEC personality type or types. Keep in mind that personality measurement is not an exact science and this fast checklist is not a scientific instrument. Nevertheless, it should give you insights that will help you understand which kinds of work in the health-care field suit you best. Use your common sense to combine the results of this exercise with other information about yourself and your work options. Talk to people who know you and are familiar with your school and work experiences.

Step 1: Respond to the Statements

Starting on the next page, carefully read each work activity. If you think you would like to do the activity, check the box next to it. (If someone else will be using this book, you should photocopy the following six pages and mark your responses on the photocopy.) Don't consider whether you have the education or training needed for it or how much money you might earn if it were part of your job. Simply decide whether you would like the activity. If you know you would dislike the activity or you're not sure, leave the box blank. After you respond to all 120 activities, you'll score your responses in Step 2.

Keep in mind that this is not a test, so there are no right or wrong answers and no time limit. Also, don't be concerned about whether an activity is in the health-care field. No matter what kinds of activities you prefer, your results will be interpreted in terms of health-care career options.

Check the boxes next to the activities you would LIKE to do.

- ❏ Build kitchen cabinets
- ❏ Guard money in an armored car
- ❏ Operate a dairy farm
- ❏ Lay brick or tile
- ❏ Monitor a machine on an assembly line
- ❏ Repair household appliances
- ❏ Drive a taxicab
- ❏ Assemble electronic parts
- ❏ Drive a truck to deliver packages to offices and homes
- ❏ Paint houses
- ❏ Enforce fish and game laws
- ❏ Work on an offshore oil-drilling rig
- ❏ Perform lawn care services
- ❏ Catch fish as a member of a fishing crew
- ❏ Refinish furniture
- ❏ Fix a broken faucet
- ❏ Do cleaning or maintenance work
- ❏ Test the quality of parts before shipment
- ❏ Operate a motorboat to carry passengers
- ❏ Put out forest fires

____ **Page score for R**

(continued)

(continued)

Check the boxes next to the activities you would LIKE to do.

- ❏ Learn about past civilizations
- ❏ Study animal behavior
- ❏ Develop a new medicine
- ❏ Discover ways to reduce water pollution
- ❏ Pinpoint the infection rate of a new disease
- ❏ Study rocks and minerals
- ❏ Diagnose and treat sick animals
- ❏ Study the personalities of world leaders
- ❏ Observe whales and other types of marine life
- ❏ Investigate crimes
- ❏ Study the movement of planets
- ❏ Examine blood samples with a microscope
- ❏ Investigate the cause of a fire
- ❏ Develop psychological profiles of criminals
- ❏ Invent a replacement for sugar
- ❏ Study genetics
- ❏ Examine the governments of different countries
- ❏ Do research on plants or animals
- ❏ Perform laboratory tests to identify diseases
- ❏ Study weather conditions

____ **Page score for I**

Check the boxes next to the activities you would LIKE to do.

- ❏ Direct a play
- ❏ Create dance routines for a show
- ❏ Write books or plays
- ❏ Play a musical instrument
- ❏ Write reviews of books or plays
- ❏ Compose or arrange music
- ❏ Act in a movie
- ❏ Dance in a Broadway show
- ❏ Draw pictures
- ❏ Create special effects for movies
- ❏ Conduct a musical choir
- ❏ Audition singers and musicians for a show
- ❏ Design sets for plays
- ❏ Announce a radio show
- ❏ Write a song
- ❏ Perform a tap or jazz dance
- ❏ Direct a movie
- ❏ Sing in a band
- ❏ Design artwork for magazines
- ❏ Pose for a photographer

____ **Page score for A**

(continued)

(continued)

Check the boxes next to the activities you would LIKE to do.

- ❑ Perform nursing duties in a hospital
- ❑ Give CPR to someone who has stopped breathing
- ❑ Help people with personal or emotional problems
- ❑ Teach children how to read
- ❑ Work with mentally disabled children
- ❑ Teach an elementary school class
- ❑ Give career guidance to people
- ❑ Supervise the activities of children at a camp
- ❑ Help people with family-related problems
- ❑ Perform rehabilitation therapy
- ❑ Help elderly people with their daily activities
- ❑ Coach children in a sport
- ❑ Teach sign language to people with hearing disabilities
- ❑ Assist people who have problems with drugs or alcohol
- ❑ Help families care for ill relatives
- ❑ Give people massages
- ❑ Plan exercises for disabled students
- ❑ Organize activities at a gym or community center
- ❑ Take care of children at a day-care center
- ❑ Teach a high school class

___ **Page score for S**

Check the boxes next to the activities you would LIKE to do.

- ❏ Buy and sell stocks and bonds
- ❏ Manage a retail store
- ❏ Operate a beauty salon or barbershop
- ❏ Sell merchandise over the telephone
- ❏ Run a stand that sells newspapers and magazines
- ❏ Give a presentation about a product you are selling
- ❏ Sell compact discs at a music store
- ❏ Manage the operations of a hotel
- ❏ Sell houses
- ❏ Manage a supermarket
- ❏ Sell a soft drink product line to stores and restaurants
- ❏ Sell refreshments at a movie theater
- ❏ Sell hair-care products to stores and salons
- ❏ Start your own business
- ❏ Negotiate business contracts
- ❏ Represent a client in a lawsuit
- ❏ Negotiate contracts for professional athletes
- ❏ Market a new line of clothing
- ❏ Sell automobiles
- ❏ Sell computer equipment in a store

____ **Page score for E**

(continued)

(continued)

Check the boxes next to the activities you would LIKE to do.

- ❏ Develop a spreadsheet using computer software
- ❏ Proofread records or forms
- ❏ Use a computer program to generate customer bills
- ❏ Schedule conferences for an organization
- ❏ Keep accounts payable/receivable for an office
- ❏ Load computer software into a large computer network
- ❏ Organize and schedule office meetings
- ❏ Use a word processor to edit and format documents
- ❏ Direct phone calls for a large organization
- ❏ File papers and records in an office
- ❏ Compute and record statistical and other numerical data
- ❏ Take notes during a meeting
- ❏ Calculate the wages of employees
- ❏ Assist senior-level accountants in performing bookkeeping tasks
- ❏ Inventory supplies using a handheld computer
- ❏ Keep records of financial transactions for an organization
- ❏ Record information from customers applying for charge accounts
- ❏ Photocopy letters and reports
- ❏ Stamp, sort, and distribute mail for an organization
- ❏ Handle customers' bank transactions

____ **Page score for C**

Step 2: Score Your Responses

To score your responses, do the following steps:

1. **Score the responses on each page.** On each page of responses, go from top to bottom and count how many boxes are checked. Then write that total on the page score line at the bottom of the page. Go on to the next page and do the same there.

2. **Determine your primary personality type.** Which page score is the highest: R, I, A, S, E, or C? Enter the letter for that personality type in the following blank. (If two page scores are tied for the highest scores or are within four points of each other, use both of them for your primary personality type. You are equally divided between two types.)

   My primary personality type: _____

3. **Determine your secondary personality types.** Which page score is the next highest? Which is your third highest score? Enter the letters for those page scores in the space provided.

   My secondary personality types: _____

Now that you know which type you are, you may be wondering what the personality types mean. Here is a short description of each one:

➤ **R (Realistic):** Realistic personalities like work activities that include practical, hands-on problems and solutions. They enjoy dealing with plants, animals, and real-world materials like wood, tools, and machinery. They enjoy outside work. Often they do not like occupations that mainly involve doing paperwork or working closely with others.

➤ **I (Investigative):** Investigative personalities like work activities that have to do with ideas and thinking more than with physical activity. They like to search for facts and figure out problems mentally rather than to persuade or lead people.

➤ **A (Artistic):** Artistic personalities like to express themselves in their work and enjoy work activities that involve artistic components such as forms, designs, and patterns. They prefer settings where they can work without following a clear set of rules.

➤ **S (Social):** Social personalities like work activities that help people and promote learning and personal development. They prefer communicating with others to working with objects, machines, or data. They like to teach, to give advice, or otherwise to be of service to people.

➤ **E (Enterprising):** Enterprising personalities like work activities having to do with starting up and carrying out projects, especially business ventures. They like persuading and leading people and making decisions. They like taking risks for profit. These personalities prefer action rather than thought.

➤ **C (Conventional):** Conventional personalities like work activities that follow set procedures and routines. They prefer working with data and details rather than with ideas. They prefer work in which there are precise standards rather than work in which you have to judge things by yourself. These personalities like working where the lines of authority are clear.

Step 3: Find Health-Care Jobs That Suit Your Personality Type

Start with your primary personality type and find matching jobs in the following table. Note that the most dominant personality type is listed first. When you find a health-care job that interests you, note the page number and turn to that page in Chapter 4, where you can read a description of that job and see the video number so you can view the video on the DVD. Don't rule out a job just because the title is not familiar to you.

If you want to find jobs that combine your primary personality type and a secondary personality type, look in the following table for RIASEC codes that match the two codes. For example, if your primary personality type is Investigative and your secondary personality type is Realistic, you would look for jobs in the table coded IR, and you'd find six, such as nuclear medicine technologists. You will also find jobs coded IR_, such as respiratory therapists (coded IRS). If you look further you'll find still more jobs coded I_R, such as pharmacists (coded ICR). All of these jobs are worth considering.

Finally, to cast an even wider net, you may want to consider *reversing* the codes you're looking for. In the current example, you might look for jobs coded RI or RI_, such as radiologic technologists (coded RIS). But you need to keep in mind that these jobs may not be quite as satisfying because your primary personality type, though represented, does not dominate. If you do not find many occupations that you like that include your primary personality type, you can use your secondary personality types to look at more career options.

HEALTH-CARE JOBS LISTED BY PERSONALITY TYPE

Occupation Name	RIASEC Code(s)	Page
Nonfarm animal caretakers	R	52
Medical appliance technicians	RI	78
Radiologic technologists	RIS	122
Veterinary assistants and laboratory animal caretakers	RIS	60
Biological technicians	RIC	98
Dental laboratory technicians	RIC	76
Medical and clinical laboratory technicians	RIC	108
Surgical technologists	RSC	96
Ophthalmic laboratory technicians	RC	70
Radiologic technicians	RCI	120
Family and general practitioners	I	176
Obstetricians and gynecologists	I	178
Pediatricians, general	I	182
Environmental scientists and specialists, including health	IR	152
Medical and clinical laboratory technologists	IR	138
Nuclear medicine technologists	IR	112
Optometrists	IR	180
Surgeons	IR	190
Veterinarians	IR	192
Cardiovascular technologists and technicians	IRS	100
Chiropractors	IRS	172
Dentists, general	IRS	174
Epidemiologists	IRS	154
Respiratory therapists	IRS	126
Clinical psychologists	IAS	168
Psychiatrists	IAS	188
Industrial safety and health engineers	IE	136
Dietitians and nutritionists	IES	134

(continued)

(continued)

HEALTH-CARE JOBS LISTED BY PERSONALITY TYPE

Occupation Name	RIASEC Code(s)	Page
Physician assistants	IS	144
Coroners	ICR	82
Forensic science technicians	ICR	106
Pharmacists	ICR	184
Athletic trainers	SR	130
Dental assistants	SR	66
Home health aides	SR	50
Nursing aides, orderlies, and attendants	SR	54
Occupational therapist assistants	SR	114
Occupational therapists	SR	160
Physical therapist aides	SR	58
Physical therapist assistants	SR	116
Emergency medical technicians and paramedics	SRI	84
Licensed practical and licensed vocational nurses	SRI	88
Physical therapists	SRI	162
Radiation therapists	SRI	118
Ambulance drivers and attendants, except emergency medical technicians	SRE	62
Animal trainers	SRE	64
Fitness trainers and aerobics instructors	SRE	86
Audiologists	SI	150
Medical and public health social workers	SI	140
Mental health counselors	SI	156
Podiatrists	SI	186
Registered nurses	SI	124
Speech-language pathologists	SI	166
Orthotists and prosthetists	SIR	142
Counseling psychologists	SIA	170

Occupation Name	RIASEC Code(s)	Page
Recreational therapists	SAR	146
Occupational health and safety specialists	SEI	158
Dental hygienists	SC	102
Medical assistants	SC	68
Social and human service assistants	SC	74
Medical and health services managers	ES	148
Opticians, dispensing	ECR	80
Medical records and health information technicians	C	110
Pharmacy technicians	CR	72
Medical secretaries	CE	92

Note: No RIASEC data is available for biomedical engineers, diagnostic medical sonographers, massage therapists, medical transcriptionists, pharmacy aides, rehabilitation counselors, and veterinary technologists and technicians, all of which are described in Chapter 4.

CHAPTER 3

Spotlight on the Best Health-Care Jobs

This chapter is designed to give you several easy ways to compare the various health-care jobs. Although this chapter ranks jobs according to which are "best" on various criteria, you should keep in mind that the best job *for you* may not be number one on any of these lists. It may not even be in the top 10. For example, ophthalmic laboratory technicians come in at the very bottom of the Best Health-Care Jobs Overall list. But that doesn't mean that this occupation is a terrible job that nobody should consider. The combination of the work tasks, the work setting, local availability of jobs, and other factors makes this job very satisfying for some people.

The lists in this chapter are ordered on the basis of economic criteria: income, job growth, and job openings. These measures are easily quantified and are often presented in lists of best jobs in the newspapers and other media. Although earnings, growth, and openings are important, there are other factors to consider in your career planning. Working in a certain location, liking the people you work with, having opportunities to be creative, and many other factors that may help define the ideal job for you are difficult or impossible to quantify and thus are not used in this book, so you will need to consider the importance of these issues yourself.

Some Details on the Lists

Using data from the U.S. Department of Labor and the Census Bureau, we followed these procedures to create the lists in this chapter:

1. We created three lists that ranked the 72 health-care jobs based on three major criteria: median annual earnings, projected growth through 2014, and number of job openings projected per year.

2. We then added the numerical ranks for each job from all three lists to calculate its overall score.

3. To emphasize jobs that tend to pay more, are likely to grow more rapidly, and have more job openings, we ordered the 72 job titles according to their numerical scores for the Best Health-Care Jobs Overall list.

4. We also created three lists that show the top 25 jobs on each of the three criteria: the 25 best-paying, the 25 fastest-growing, and the 25 with the most job openings.

Note that although dental hygienists rank first on the Best Health-Care Jobs Overall list because this occupation has the best combined score for earnings, growth, and number of job openings, it is not the best-paying job (which is a tie between three physician jobs), the fastest-growing job (which is home health aides), or the job with the most openings (which is nursing aides, orderlies, and attendants).

When you compare jobs on the lists, keep in mind that some jobs have the same combined scores. For example, in the Best Health-Care Jobs Overall list, the top five jobs *all have the same combined score*. Dental hygienists are listed first only because that is where this job falls under alphabetical ordering. The next three jobs are related physician jobs with identical scores, and registered nurses come in at fourth place, also with the identical score. Similarly, the jobs ranked 20, 21, and 22 have the same score. There was no way to avoid these ties, so simply understand that the difference of several positions on a list may not mean as much as it seems.

In addition, some jobs share certain data elements. For example, in Chapter 4 you will find separate descriptions of radiologic technologists and radiologic technicians, so you will also find these as two separate jobs on the lists in this chapter. However, the U.S. Department of Labor provides data only for the single combined job called radiologic technologists and technicians, which means that on these lists we have to print the same economic information for both jobs. This information can be misleading if you don't understand that the data comes from both jobs. For example, the figure of 23.2 percent for their job growth is an average. Probably one of these jobs is growing faster than the other, but we don't have separate figures. It's especially important to understand that the figure of 17,000 job openings represents the *total* number of job openings for the two jobs. They share this figure—each job is projected to have *some fraction* of 17,000 job openings, but we don't know exactly how many. To remind you about how to read these figures, we identify all the jobs that share data in footnotes after each list that contains such jobs.

Finally, note that the earnings figures are based on the average annual pay received by full-time workers. Because the earnings represent the national averages, actual pay rates can vary greatly by location, amount of previous work experience, and other factors. Earnings of self-employed workers are not counted in these averages, and self-employment is a fairly common work arrangement in a few health-care jobs.

The Best Health-Care Jobs Lists

The Best Health-Care Jobs Overall list is the one that most people want to see first. It orders the 72 health-care jobs according to their overall combined ratings for earnings, projected growth, and number of openings. As noted previously, many jobs had tied scores and are simply listed one after another, so there are often only very small or even no differences between the scores of jobs that are near each other on the list. You can find descriptions for each of these jobs in Chapter 4.

THE BEST HEALTH-CARE JOBS OVERALL

Rank and Job Title	Annual Earnings	Percent Growth	Annual Openings
1. Dental hygienists	$60,890	43.3%	17,000
2. Obstetricians and gynecologists	More than $145,600	24.0%	41,000
3. Psychiatrists	More than $145,600	24.0%	41,000
4. Surgeons	More than $145,600	24.0%	41,000
5. Registered nurses	$54,670	29.4%	229,000
6. Family and general practitioners	$140,400	24.0%	41,000
7. Pediatricians, general	$136,600	24.0%	41,000
8. Physician assistants	$72,030	49.6%	10,000
9. Physical therapists	$63,080	36.7%	13,000
10. Pharmacists	$89,820	24.6%	16,000
11. Dental assistants	$29,520	42.7%	45,000
12. Medical assistants	$25,350	52.1%	93,000
13. Medical and health services managers	$69,700	22.8%	33,000
14. Home health aides	$18,800	56.0%	170,000
15. Occupational therapists	$56,860	33.6%	7,000
16. Diagnostic medical sonographers	$54,370	34.8%	5,000

(continued)

THE BEST HEALTH-CARE JOBS OVERALL

Rank and Job Title	Annual Earnings	Percent Growth	Annual Openings
17. Social and human service assistants	$25,030	29.7%	61,000
18. Physical therapist assistants	$39,490	44.2%	7,000
19. Biomedical engineers	$71,840	30.7%	1,000
20. Fitness trainers and aerobics instructors	$25,840	27.1%	50,000
21. Medical and public health social workers	$41,120	25.9%	14,000
22. Surgical technologists	$34,830	29.5%	12,000
23. Radiologic technicians	$45,950	23.2%	17,000
24. Radiologic technologists	$45,950	23.2%	17,000
25. Mental health counselors	$34,010	27.2%	14,000
26. Emergency medical technicians and paramedics	$26,080	27.3%	21,000
27. Respiratory therapists	$45,140	28.4%	7,000
28. Cardiovascular technologists and technicians	$40,420	32.6%	5,000
29. Pharmacy technicians	$24,390	28.6%	35,000
30. Medical records and health information technicians	$26,690	28.9%	14,000
31. Forensic science technicians	$44,590	36.4%	2,000
32. Licensed practical and licensed vocational nurses	$35,230	17.1%	84,000
33. Clinical psychologists	$57,170	19.1%	10,000
34. Counseling psychologists	$57,170	19.1%	10,000
35. Medical and clinical laboratory technologists	$47,710	20.5%	14,000
36. Medical and clinical laboratory technicians	$31,700	25.0%	14,000
37. Veterinary technologists and technicians	$25,670	35.3%	9,000
38. Radiation therapists	$62,340	26.3%	1,000
39. Veterinarians	$68,910	17.4%	8,000
40. Chiropractors	$67,200	22.4%	4,000

Rank and Job Title	Annual Earnings	Percent Growth	Annual Openings
41. Medical transcriptionists	$29,080	23.3%	20,000
42. Occupational therapist assistants	$39,750	34.1%	2,000
43. Dentists, general	$125,300	13.5%	7,000
44. Nursing aides, orderlies, and attendants	$21,440	22.3%	307,000
45. Rehabilitation counselors	$28,330	23.9%	19,000
46. Optometrists	$88,040	19.7%	2,000
47. Nonfarm animal caretakers	$17,720	25.6%	31,000
48. Coroners	$49,360	11.6%	17,000
49. Massage therapists	$32,890	23.6%	12,000
50. Epidemiologists	$52,170	26.2%	1,000
51. Medical secretaries	$27,320	17.0%	55,000
52. Nuclear medicine technologists	$59,670	21.5%	2,000
53. Physical therapist aides	$21,510	34.4%	5,000
54. Environmental scientists and specialists, including health	$52,630	17.1%	8,000
55. Athletic trainers	$34,260	29.3%	1,000
56. Podiatrists	$100,550	16.2%	1,000
57. Speech-language pathologists	$54,880	14.6%	5,000
58. Industrial safety and health engineers	$65,210	13.4%	2,000
59. Biological technicians	$34,270	17.2%	8,000
60. Veterinary assistants and laboratory animal caretakers	$19,610	21.0%	14,000
61. Ambulance drivers and attendants, except emergency medical technicians	$18,790	28.0%	5,000
62. Dietitians and nutritionists	$44,940	18.3%	4,000
63. Occupational health and safety specialists	$53,710	12.4%	3,000
64. Orthotists and prosthetists	$53,760	18.0%	Fewer than 500
65. Pharmacy aides	$18,900	17.4%	9,000
66. Opticians, dispensing	$29,000	13.6%	6,000

(continued)

(continued)

THE BEST HEALTH-CARE JOBS OVERALL

Rank and Job Title	Annual Earnings	Percent Growth	Annual Openings
67. Animal trainers	$24,800	20.3%	3,000
68. Audiologists	$53,490	9.1%	Fewer than 500
69. Recreational therapists	$33,480	5.7%	3,000
70. Dental laboratory technicians	$32,240	7.6%	3,000
71. Medical appliance technicians	$29,080	13.2%	1,000
72. Ophthalmic laboratory technicians	$24,740	7.8%	2,000

Jobs 2, 3, 4, 6, and 7 share 41,000 openings with each other and with two other jobs not included in this list. Jobs 23 and 24 share 17,000 openings. Jobs 33 and 34 share 10,000 openings. Job 48 shares 17,000 openings with four other jobs not included in this list. Job 58 shares 2,000 openings with two other jobs not included in this list.

The following list shows the 25 best-paying health-care jobs. Their average earnings (a mean of the median earnings, weighted to represent the size of the workforce of each job) are about $65,600, which compares very favorably to the average of $29,430 for all occupations in the U.S. economy.

THE BEST-PAYING HEALTH-CARE JOBS

Rank and Job Title	Annual Earnings
1. Obstetricians and gynecologists	More than $145,600
2. Psychiatrists	More than $145,600
3. Surgeons	More than $145,600
4. Family and general practitioners	$140,400
5. Pediatricians, general	$136,600
6. Dentists, general	$125,300
7. Podiatrists	$100,550
8. Pharmacists	$89,820
9. Optometrists	$88,040
10. Physician assistants	$72,030
11. Biomedical engineers	$71,840
12. Medical and health services managers	$69,700

Rank and Job Title	Annual Earnings
13. Veterinarians	$68,910
14. Chiropractors	$67,200
15. Industrial safety and health engineers	$65,210
16. Physical therapists	$63,080
17. Radiation therapists	$62,340
18. Dental hygienists	$60,890
19. Nuclear medicine technologists	$59,670
20. Clinical psychologists	$57,170
21. Counseling psychologists	$57,170
22. Occupational therapists	$56,860
23. Speech-language pathologists	$54,880
24. Registered nurses	$54,670
25. Diagnostic medical sonographers	$54,370

The next list shows the 25 fastest-growing health-care jobs. Their average (mean) rate of growth, 35.3 percent, is almost *triple* the average growth of all occupations, 13.0 percent.

THE FASTEST-GROWING HEALTH-CARE JOBS

Rank and Job Title	Percent Growth
1. Home health aides	56.0%
2. Medical assistants	52.1%
3. Physician assistants	49.6%
4. Physical therapist assistants	44.2%
5. Dental hygienists	43.3%
6. Dental assistants	42.7%
7. Physical therapists	36.7%
8. Forensic science technicians	36.4%
9. Veterinary technologists and technicians	35.3%
10. Diagnostic medical sonographers	34.8%

(continued)

THE FASTEST-GROWING HEALTH-CARE JOBS

Rank and Job Title	Percent Growth
11. Physical therapist aides	34.4%
12. Occupational therapist assistants	34.1%
13. Occupational therapists	33.6%
14. Cardiovascular technologists and technicians	32.6%
15. Biomedical engineers	30.7%
16. Social and human service assistants	29.7%
17. Surgical technologists	29.5%
18. Registered nurses	29.4%
19. Athletic trainers	29.3%
20. Medical records and health information technicians	28.9%
21. Pharmacy technicians	28.6%
22. Respiratory therapists	28.4%
23. Ambulance drivers and attendants, except emergency medical technicians	28.0%
24. Emergency medical technicians and paramedics	27.3%
25. Mental health counselors	27.2%

The final list shows the 25 health-care jobs with the most job openings. Their average (mean) number of openings, about 61,600, is almost twice the average for all jobs, 34,600.

THE HEALTH-CARE JOBS WITH THE MOST OPENINGS

Rank and Job Title	Annual Openings
1. Nursing aides, orderlies, and attendants	307,000
2. Registered nurses	229,000
3. Home health aides	170,000
4. Medical assistants	93,000
5. Licensed practical and licensed vocational nurses	84,000
6. Social and human service assistants	61,000

Rank and Job Title	Annual Openings
7. Medical secretaries	55,000
8. Fitness trainers and aerobics instructors	50,000
9. Dental assistants	45,000
10. Family and general practitioners	41,000
11. Obstetricians and gynecologists	41,000
12. Pediatricians, general	41,000
13. Psychiatrists	41,000
14. Surgeons	41,000
15. Pharmacy technicians	35,000
16. Medical and health services managers	33,000
17. Nonfarm animal caretakers	31,000
18. Emergency medical technicians and paramedics	21,000
19. Medical transcriptionists	20,000
20. Rehabilitation counselors	19,000
21. Coroners	17,000
22. Dental hygienists	17,000
23. Radiologic technicians	17,000
24. Radiologic technologists	17,000
25. Pharmacists	16,000

Jobs 10, 11, 12, 13, and 14 share 41,000 openings with each other and with two other jobs not included in this list. Job 21 shares 17,000 openings with four other jobs not included in this list. Jobs 23 and 24 share 17,000 openings.

Health-Care Careers in Focus

This chapter describes each of the 72 health-care jobs on the DVD, using a format that is informative yet compact and easy to read. The job descriptions in this chapter are arranged by level of education or training required and within each level by alphabetical order. This arrangement makes it easy to find jobs with a level of preparation that you're willing to consider. Each job description contains statistics such as earnings and projected percent of growth; lists such as major work tasks, skills, and work environment; and key descriptors such as personality type and interest field.

If you are using this chapter to browse for interesting options, we suggest you begin with the Table of Contents, which lists all the job titles in this chapter. If you have not browsed the lists in Chapter 3, consider spending some time there as well. The lists are interesting and will help you identify job titles to learn more about. Consider the job descriptions in this section and the videos on the DVD as the first steps in career exploration.

You may notice that statements in the book occasionally differ with the information in the videos. This happens because we were able to use up-to-the-minute information in the book based on the latest government data.

Education and Training Levels

The health-care jobs in this book are grouped into 11 different levels of education and training, starting with the Short-Term On-the-Job Training section and ending with the First Professional Degree section. The tabs along the side of the job descriptions pages indicate the education and training level for each group of job descriptions. The following text explains each of these levels and lists the jobs in each level.

SHORT-TERM ON-THE-JOB TRAINING

In the jobs described in the Short-Term On-the-Job Training section, a worker can achieve an average level of performance within a few days or weeks through on-the-job training. The following jobs are included in this section:

➤ Home health aides

➤ Nonfarm animal caretakers

➤ Nursing aides, orderlies, and attendants

➤ Pharmacy aides

➤ Physical therapist aides

➤ Veterinary assistants and laboratory animal caretakers

MODERATE-TERM ON-THE-JOB TRAINING

The jobs described in the Moderate-Term On-the-Job Training section can be performed adequately after a period of 1 to 12 months of combined on-the-job and informal training. Typically, untrained workers observe experienced workers performing tasks and are assigned progressively more responsible tasks as they acquire job-related skills.

This section includes the following jobs:

➤ Ambulance drivers and attendants, except emergency medical technicians

➤ Animal trainers

➤ Dental assistants

➤ Medical assistants

➤ Ophthalmic laboratory technicians

➤ Pharmacy technicians

➤ Social and human service assistants

LONG-TERM ON-THE-JOB TRAINING

The jobs described in the Long-Term On-the-Job Training section require more than 12 months of on-the-job training or combined work experience and formal classroom instruction. This group includes occupations that use formal apprenticeships for training workers that may take up to four years. The following jobs are included in this section:

➤ Dental laboratory technicians

➤ Medical appliance technicians

➤ Opticians, dispensing

WORK EXPERIENCE IN A RELATED OCCUPATION

The Work Experience in a Related Occupation section has one job: coroner. Many coroners have work experience as physicians.

POSTSECONDARY VOCATIONAL TRAINING

The jobs described in the Postsecondary Vocational Training section require formal preparation that can vary from training that involves a few months to usually less than one year. In a few instances, there may be as many as four years of training. The following jobs are included in this section:

➤ Emergency medical technicians and paramedics

➤ Fitness trainers and aerobics instructors

➤ Licensed practical and licensed vocational nurses

➤ Massage therapists

➤ Medical secretaries

➤ Medical transcriptionists

➤ Surgical technologists

ASSOCIATE DEGREE

The jobs described in the Associate Degree section usually require two years of full-time academic work beyond high school. This section includes the following jobs:

➤ Biological technicians

➤ Cardiovascular technologists and technicians

➤ Dental hygienists

- ➤ Diagnostic medical sonographers
- ➤ Forensic science technicians
- ➤ Medical and clinical laboratory technicians
- ➤ Medical records and health information technicians
- ➤ Nuclear medicine technologists
- ➤ Occupational therapist assistants
- ➤ Physical therapist assistants
- ➤ Radiation therapists
- ➤ Radiologic technicians
- ➤ Radiologic technologists
- ➤ Registered nurses
- ➤ Respiratory therapists
- ➤ Veterinary technologists and technicians

BACHELOR'S DEGREE

The jobs described in the Bachelor's Degree section require approximately four to five years of full-time academic work beyond high school. The following jobs are included in this section:

- ➤ Athletic trainers
- ➤ Biomedical engineers
- ➤ Dietitians and nutritionists
- ➤ Industrial safety and health engineers
- ➤ Medical and clinical laboratory technologists
- ➤ Medical and public health social workers
- ➤ Orthotists and prosthetists
- ➤ Physician assistants
- ➤ Recreational therapists

WORK EXPERIENCE PLUS DEGREE

The job described in the Work Experience Plus Degree section, medical and health services managers, requires some experience in a related nonmanagerial position in addition to a bachelor's or master's degree.

MASTER'S DEGREE

The jobs described in the Master's Degree section usually require one to two years of full-time study beyond the bachelor's degree. This section includes the following jobs:

➤ Audiologists

➤ Environmental scientists and specialists, including health

➤ Epidemiologists

➤ Mental health counselors

➤ Occupational health and safety specialists

➤ Occupational therapists

➤ Physical therapists

➤ Rehabilitation counselors

➤ Speech-language pathologists

DOCTORAL DEGREE

The two jobs described in the Doctoral Degree section, clinical psychologists and counseling psychologists, normally require five to seven years of full-time academic work beyond the bachelor's degree, including at least one year of internship.

FIRST PROFESSIONAL DEGREE

The jobs described in the First Professional Degree section normally require a minimum of two years of education beyond the bachelor's degree and frequently require three or more years. The academic programs all include clinical training, and physician jobs also require an internship. The following jobs are included in this section:

➤ Chiropractors

➤ Dentists, general

➤ Family and general practitioners

➤ Obstetricians and gynecologists

➤ Optometrists

➤ Pediatricians, general

➤ Pharmacists

➤ Podiatrists

➤ Psychiatrists

➤ Surgeons

➤ Veterinarians

The Job Descriptions

To create the job descriptions, we gathered the most current information from a variety of government sources. (The sources are identified in detail in Appendix B.) The results of this complicated process are not always perfect, but we think that they will be helpful to many people. Although we've tried to make the descriptions easy to understand, the following explanation of each of the parts may help you better understand and use the descriptions.

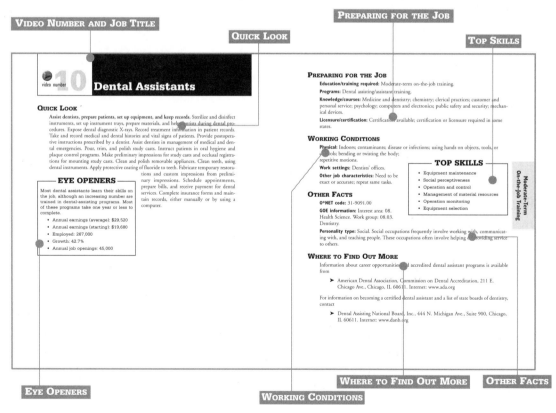

VIDEO NUMBER AND JOB TITLE

QUICK LOOK

PREPARING FOR THE JOB

TOP SKILLS

video number **10** **Dental Assistants**

QUICK LOOK

Assist dentists, prepare patients, set up equipment, and keep records. Sterilize and disinfect instruments, set up instrument trays, prepare materials, and help dentists during dental procedures. Expose dental diagnostic X-rays. Record treatment information in patient records. Take and record medical and dental histories and vital signs of patients. Provide postoperative instructions prescribed by a dentist. Assist dentists in management of medical and dental emergencies. Pour, trim, and polish study casts. Instruct patients in oral hygiene and plaque control programs. Make preliminary impressions for study casts and occlusal registrations for mounting study casts. Clean and polish removable appliances. Clean teeth, using dental instruments. Apply protective coating of fluoride to teeth. Fabricate temporary restorations and custom impressions from preliminary impressions. Schedule appointments, prepare bills, and receive payment for dental services. Complete insurance forms and maintain records, either manually or by using a computer.

EYE OPENERS

Most dental assistants learn their skills on the job, although an increasing number are trained in dental-assisting programs. Most of these programs take one year or less to complete.

- Annual earnings (average): $29,520
- Annual earnings (starting): $19,680
- Employed: 267,000
- Growth: 42.7%
- Annual job openings: 45,000

PREPARING FOR THE JOB

Education/training required: Moderate-term on-the-job training.

Programs: Dental assisting/assistant training.

Knowledge/courses: Medicine and dentistry; chemistry; clerical practices; customer and personal service; psychology; computers and electronics; public safety and security; mechanical devices.

Licensure/certification: Certification available; certification or licensure required in some states.

WORKING CONDITIONS

Physical: Indoors; contaminants; disease or infections; using hands on objects, tools, or controls; bending or twisting the body; repetitive motions.

Work settings: Dentists' offices.

Other job characteristics: Need to be exact or accurate; repeat same tasks.

OTHER FACTS

O*NET code: 31-9091.00

GOE information: Interest area: 08. Health Science. Work group: 08.03. Dentistry.

Personality type: Social. Social occupations frequently involve working with, communicating with, and teaching people. These occupations often involve helping or providing service to others.

WHERE TO FIND OUT MORE

Information about career opportunities and accredited dental assistant programs is available from

➤ American Dental Association, Commission on Dental Accreditation, 211 E. Chicago Ave., Chicago, IL 60611. Internet: www.ada.org

For information on becoming a certified dental assistant and a list of state boards of dentistry, contact

➤ Dental Assisting National Board, Inc., 444 N. Michigan Ave., Suite 900, Chicago, IL 60611. Internet: www.danb.org

TOP SKILLS

- Equipment maintenance
- Social perceptiveness
- Operation and control
- Management of material resources
- Operation monitoring
- Equipment selection

Moderate-Term On-the-Job Training

EYE OPENERS

WORKING CONDITIONS

WHERE TO FIND OUT MORE

OTHER FACTS

Video Number and Job Title

Each job description begins by listing the video number and the job title. The video number lets you easily find the appropriate video on the DVD. The job title is the title for the job as defined by the U.S. Department of Labor and used in its O*NET (Occupational Information Network) database. This database is the Department of Labor's official source of occupational data. In four cases, the title used in the video is slightly different from the title of the job. In two cases, a single video describes two jobs, so that video is on the DVD twice.

Quick Look

The bold sentences in the Quick Look part provide a summary description of the job. This description is followed by a listing of tasks that are generally performed by people who work in this job. This information comes from the O*NET database, but we have edited it for length where necessary.

Eye Openers

The Eye Openers box highlights key facts about the job. These facts include information about earnings, rate of job growth, and number of openings. The information comes from various U.S. Department of Labor and Census Bureau databases, as explained in detail in Appendix B.

Preparing for the Job

The Preparing for the Job part of the job description provides the amount of education or training required for the job; the name of the academic or training programs often recommended as preparation for this job; the kinds of knowledge commonly needed on the job, which reflect the courses commonly taken as part of the preparation program; and whether a license or certificate is required or available for the job. This information will help you identify sources of formal or informal training and any other prerequisites for job entry.

Top Skills

The Top Skills box is based on skills-related data from the O*NET database. For each skill and each job, O*NET gives two ratings: one for the level of skill needed, and one for the importance of the skill. The skills listed in the Top Skills box are those whose level-of-performance scores exceed the average for all jobs by the greatest amount and whose ratings on the importance scale are not very low. We include as many as six such skills for each job, and we rank them by the extent to which their rating exceeds the average. This section can help you recognize whether you can meet the skill requirements of the job. It also can suggest skills that will be useful to include in your resume when you hunt for a job opening in this occupation. For definitions of the skills, see Appendix C.

WORKING CONDITIONS

If you have a strong preference or dislike for certain work environments, you may find the information in the Working Conditions part helpful. This part includes three main components:

➤ **Physical:** The work conditions we include are derived from a set of 23 covered by the O*NET database. We list any whose rating exceeds the midpoint of the rating scale. The ordering of the work conditions does not reflect importance. Instead, we try to keep logically related conditions together. Keep in mind that when hazards are present (for example, radiation), protective equipment and procedures are provided to keep you safe.

➤ **Work settings:** This information identifies the specific locations, such as hospitals and doctors' offices, where the job is most often performed.

➤ **Other job characteristics:** These items are conditions that the O*NET database calls "structural." These are characteristics such as the need for accuracy or the likelihood of repetition. For each job, we include any characteristics from this set whose score exceeds the midpoint of the rating scale, and we rank them in descending order of importance.

OTHER FACTS

The Other Facts part lists the following facts that will help you explore the job further and understand its relationship to other jobs:

➤ **O*NET code:** This code is used in many other sources that you may consult. Jobs beginning with the same two digits are assigned to the same family of jobs in the Standard Occupational Classification scheme used by the federal government.

➤ **GOE information:** This information cross-references the Guide for Occupational Exploration, a system developed by the U.S. Department of Labor that organizes jobs based on interests. We use the groups from the *New Guide for Occupational Exploration*, Fourth Edition, as published by JIST. This book uses a set of interest areas based on the 16 career clusters developed by the U.S. Department of Education and used in a variety of career information systems. The description includes the major interest area the job fits into and its more-specific work group. This information will help you identify other job titles that have similar interests or require similar skills. To understand the context of the GOE work groups referred to in the descriptions, turn to Appendix D. There you will find a complete listing of the GOE interest areas and work groups.

➤ **Personality type:** This type tells you where the job is located in the RIASEC classification devised by John L. Holland. You can find more information on the RIASEC personality types in the introduction to the checklist exercise in Chapter 2.

WHERE TO FIND OUT MORE

No single book, even when accompanied by a DVD, can tell you everything you need to know to make a career decision. The Where to Find Out More part of each job description suggests resources for learning more about that job. In Appendix E, we identify several additional resources that provide information about multiple occupations or can help with making career decisions or hunting for jobs. Before you make a career decision, take the time to investigate your options thoroughly.

Home Health Aides

QUICK LOOK

Provide routine, personal health care, such as bathing, dressing, or grooming, to elderly, convalescent, or disabled persons in their homes or in a residential care facility. Maintain records of patient care, condition, progress, or problems to report and discuss observations with supervisor or case manager. Provide patients with help moving in and out of beds, bathtubs, wheelchairs, or automobiles and with dressing and grooming. Provide patients and families with emotional support and instruction in areas such as caring for infants, preparing healthy meals, living independently, or adapting to a disability or illness. Change bed linens, wash and iron patients' laundry, and clean patients' quarters. Entertain, converse with, or read aloud to patients to keep them mentally healthy and alert. Plan, purchase, prepare, or serve meals to patients or other family members according to prescribed diets. Direct patients in simple prescribed exercises or in the use of braces or artificial limbs. Check the pulse, temperature, and respiration of patients. Change dressings. Perform a variety of duties as requested by client, such as obtaining household supplies or running errands. Accompany clients to physicians' offices and on other trips outside the home, providing transportation, assistance, and companionship. Administer prescribed oral medications under written direction of physician or as directed by home care nurse and aide. Care for children who are disabled or who have sick or disabled parents. Massage patients and apply preparations and treatments such as liniment, alcohol rubs, and heat-lamp stimulation.

— EYE OPENERS —

This job is projected to be the fastest-growing occupation through 2014.

- Annual earnings (average): $18,800
- Annual earnings (starting): $14,140
- Employed: 624,000
- Growth: 56.0%
- Annual job openings: 170,000

PREPARING FOR THE JOB

Education/training required: Short-term on-the-job training.

Programs: Home health aide/home attendant training.

Knowledge/courses: Medicine and dentistry; therapy and counseling; psychology.

Licensure/certification: Certification available.

WORKING CONDITIONS

Physical: Indoors; disease or infections; standing; walking and running; repetitive motions.

Work settings: Clients' homes, often at multiple locations on the same day.

Other job characteristics: Need to be exact or accurate; errors have important consequences.

OTHER FACTS

O*NET code: 31-1011.00

GOE information: Interest area: 08. Health Science. Work group: 08.08. Patient Care and Assistance.

Personality type: Social. Social occupations frequently involve working with, communicating with, and teaching people. These occupations often involve helping or providing service to others.

── TOP SKILLS ──

- Social perceptiveness

WHERE TO FIND OUT MORE

Information about employment opportunities may be obtained from local hospitals, nursing care facilities, home health-care agencies, psychiatric facilities, state boards of nursing, and local offices of the state employment service. Information on licensing requirements for nursing and home health aides and lists of state-approved nursing aide programs are available from state departments of public health, departments of occupational licensing, boards of nursing, and home care associations.

Additional information is available from

➤ National Association for Home Care & Hospice, 228 7th St. SE, Washington, DC 20003. Internet: www.nahc.org/

Nonfarm Animal Caretakers

QUICK LOOK

Care for pets and other nonfarm animals, such as dogs, cats, ornamental fish or birds, zoo animals, and mice in settings such as kennels, animal shelters, zoos, circuses, and aquariums. Feed and water animals according to schedules and feeding instructions. Clean, organize, disinfect, and repair animal quarters such as pens, stables, cages, fish tanks, and yards and animal equipment such as saddles and bridles. Answer telephones and schedule appointments. Examine and observe animals to detect signs of illness, disease, or injury. Respond to questions from patrons and provide information about animals, such as behavior, habitat, breeding habits, or facility activities. Provide treatment to sick or injured animals or contact veterinarians to secure treatment. Collect and record animal information such as weight, size, physical condition, treatments received, medications given, and food intake. Keep records of animals received or discharged. Perform animal grooming duties such as washing, brushing, clipping, and trimming coats; cutting nails; and cleaning ears. Exercise animals to maintain their physical and mental health. Order, unload, and store feed and supplies. Mix food, liquid formulas, medications, or food supplements according to instructions, prescriptions, and knowledge of animal species. Clean and disinfect surgical equipment. Discuss with clients their pets' grooming needs. Observe and caution children petting and feeding animals in designated areas to ensure the safety of humans and animals. Find homes for stray or unwanted animals. Adjust controls to regulate specified temperature and humidity of animal quarters, nurseries, or exhibit areas. Anesthetize and inoculate animals, according to instructions. Transfer animals between enclosures to facilitate breeding, birthing, shipping, or rearrangement of exhibits. Install, maintain, and repair animal care facility equipment such as infrared lights, feeding devices, and cages. Train animals to perform certain tasks. Teach obedience classes. Sell pet food and supplies. Saddle and shoe animals.

EYE OPENERS

Animal lovers get satisfaction in this occupation, but the work can be unpleasant, physically and emotionally demanding, and sometimes dangerous.

- Annual earnings (average): $17,720
- Annual earnings (starting): $13,380
- Employed: 128,000
- Growth: 25.6%
- Annual job openings: 31,000

PREPARING FOR THE JOB

Education/training required: Short-term on-the-job training.

Programs: Agricultural/farm supplies retailing and wholesaling; dog/pet/animal grooming.

Knowledge/courses: Customer and personal service.

Licensure/certification: Certification available.

WORKING CONDITIONS

Physical: More often outdoors than indoors; noisy; contaminants; minor burns, cuts, bites, or stings; standing.

Work settings: Kennels, pet stores, animal hospitals, research facilities, and animal shelters.

Other job characteristics: Need to be exact or accurate.

OTHER FACTS

O*NET code: 39-2021.00

GOE information: Interest area: 08. Health Science. Work group: 08.05. Animal Care.

Personality type: Realistic. Realistic occupations frequently involve work activities that include practical, hands-on problems and solutions. They often deal with plants, animals, and real-world materials like wood, tools, and machinery. Many of the occupations require working outside and do not involve a lot of paperwork or working closely with others.

TOP SKILLS

- Time management
- Management of financial resources
- Social perceptiveness
- Equipment maintenance
- Management of material resources

WHERE TO FIND OUT MORE

For career information and information on training, certification, and earnings of animal control officers at federal, state, and local levels, contact

➤ National Animal Control Association, P.O. Box 1480851, Kansas City, MO 64148-0851. Internet: www.nacanet.org/

For information on becoming an advanced pet care technician at a kennel, contact

➤ American Boarding Kennels Association, 1702 E. Pikes Peak Ave., Colorado Springs, CO 80909. Internet: www.abka.com

video number 4

Nursing Aides, Orderlies, and Attendants

QUICK LOOK

Provide basic patient care under the direction of nursing staff in hospitals and other health-care facilities. Turn and reposition bedridden patients, alone or with assistance, to prevent bedsores. Answer patients' call signals. Feed patients who are unable to feed themselves. Observe patients' conditions, measuring and recording food and liquid intake and output and vital signs, and report changes to professional staff. Provide patient care by supplying and emptying bedpans, applying dressings, and supervising exercise routines. Provide patients with help walking, exercising, and moving in and out of bed. Bathe, groom, shave, dress, or drape patients to prepare them for surgery, treatment, or examination. Collect specimens such as urine, feces, or sputum. Prepare, serve, and collect food trays. Clean rooms and change linens. Transport patients to treatment units by using a wheelchair or stretcher. Deliver messages, documents, and specimens. Answer phones and direct visitors. Administer medications and treatments, such as catheterizations, suppositories, irrigations, enemas, massages, and douches, as directed by a physician or nurse. Restrain patients if necessary. Maintain inventory by storing, preparing, sterilizing, and issuing supplies such as dressing packs and treatment trays. Explain medical instructions to patients and family members. Perform clerical duties such as processing documents and scheduling appointments. Work as part of a medical team that examines and treats clinic outpatients. Set up equipment such as oxygen tents, portable X-ray machines, and overhead irrigation bottles.

— EYE OPENERS —

Numerous job openings and excellent job opportunities are expected for this occupation.

- Annual earnings (average): $21,440
- Annual earnings (starting): $15,580
- Employed: 1,455,000
- Growth: 22.3%
- Annual job openings: 307,000

PREPARING FOR THE JOB

Education/training required: Short-term on-the-job training.

Programs: Health aide training; nurse/nursing assistant/aide and patient care assistant training.

Knowledge/courses: Psychology; medicine and dentistry; customer and personal service; chemistry; English language; education and training.

Licensure/certification: Certification available.

WORKING CONDITIONS

Physical: Indoors; disease or infections; standing; walking and running; using hands on objects, tools, or controls; bending or twisting the body.

Work settings: Hospitals and other health-care facilities.

Other job characteristics: Need to be exact or accurate; errors have important consequences; repeat same tasks.

─── TOP SKILLS ───

- Social perceptiveness
- Operation monitoring
- Time management
- Service orientation
- Monitoring
- Instructing

OTHER FACTS

O*NET code: 31-1012.00

GOE information: Interest area: 08. Health Science. Work group: 08.08. Patient Care and Assistance.

Personality type: Social. Social occupations frequently involve working with, communicating with, and teaching people. These occupations often involve helping or providing service to others.

WHERE TO FIND OUT MORE

Information about employment opportunities may be obtained from local hospitals, nursing care facilities, home health-care agencies, psychiatric facilities, state boards of nursing, and local offices of the state employment service.

Information on licensing requirements for nursing and home health aides and lists of state-approved nursing aide programs are available from state departments of public health, departments of occupational licensing, boards of nursing, and home care associations.

Additional information is available from

➤ National Association for Home Care & Hospice, 228 7th St. SE, Washington, DC 20003. Internet: www.nahc.org/

Pharmacy Aides

QUICK LOOK

Record drugs delivered to the pharmacy, store incoming merchandise, and inform the supervisor of stock needs. May operate cash register and accept prescriptions for filling. Gather and process necessary information for filling prescriptions. Answer telephone inquiries, referring callers to pharmacist when necessary. Prepare solid and liquid dosage medications for dispensing into bottles and unit dose packaging. Greet customers and help them locate merchandise. Unpack, sort, count, and label incoming merchandise, including items requiring special handling or refrigeration. Prepare prescription labels by typing or operating a computer and printer. Receive, store, and inventory pharmaceutical supplies, notifying pharmacist when levels are low. Operate cash register to process cash and credit sales. Restock storage areas, replenishing items on shelves. Perform clerical tasks such as filing, compiling and maintaining prescription records, and composing letters. Maintain and clean equipment, work areas, and shelves. Provide customers with information about the uses and effects of drugs. Prepare and maintain records of inventories, receipts, purchases, and deliveries, using a variety of computer screen formats. Process medical insurance claims, posting bill amounts and calculating co-payments. Compound, package, and label pharmaceutical products under the direction of a pharmacist. Operate a capsule- and tablet-counting machine that automatically distributes a certain number of capsules or tablets into smaller containers. Calculate anticipated drug usage for a prescribed period. Deliver medication to treatment areas, living units, residences, and clinics, using various means of transportation.

── EYE OPENERS ──

Job opportunities for pharmacy aides are expected to be good for full-time and part-time work, especially for those with related work experience.

- Annual earnings (average): $18,900
- Annual earnings (starting): $13,850
- Employed: 50,000
- Growth: 17.4%
- Annual job openings: 9,000

PREPARING FOR THE JOB

Education/training required: Short-term on-the-job training.

Programs: Pharmacy technician/assistant training.

Knowledge/courses: Medicine and dentistry; clerical practices; customer and personal service; chemistry; economics and accounting; computers and electronics; production and processing; mathematics.

Licensure/certification: Not relevant.

WORKING CONDITIONS

Physical: Indoors; disease or infections; standing; walking and running; using hands on objects, tools, or controls; repetitive motions.

Work settings: Hospitals and retail pharmacies.

Other job characteristics: Need to be exact or accurate; repeat same tasks; errors have important consequences.

OTHER FACTS

O*NET code: 31-9095.00

GOE information: Interest area: 08. Health Science. Work group: 08.02. Medicine and Surgery.

Personality type: No data available.

TOP SKILLS

- Operation and control
- Service orientation
- Judgment and decision making
- Systems evaluation
- Active learning
- Learning strategies

WHERE TO FIND OUT MORE

For information on employment opportunities, contact local employers or local offices of the state employment service.

Physical Therapist Aides

QUICK LOOK

Under close supervision of a physical therapist or physical therapy assistant, perform only delegated, selected, or routine tasks in specific situations. These duties include preparing the patient and the treatment area. Clean and organize work area and disinfect equipment after treatment. Observe patients during treatment to compile and evaluate data on patients' responses and progress and report to physical therapist. Instruct, motivate, safeguard, and assist patients practicing exercises and functional activities under direction of medical staff. Secure patients into or onto therapy equipment. Transport patients to and from treatment areas, using wheelchairs or providing standing support. Confer with physical therapy staff or others to discuss and evaluate patient information for planning, modifying, and coordinating treatment. Record treatment given and equipment used. Perform clerical duties, such as taking inventory, ordering supplies, answering telephones, taking messages, and filling out forms. Maintain equipment and furniture to keep it in good working condition, including assembling and disassembling equipment and accessories. Administer active and passive manual therapeutic exercises; therapeutic massage; and heat, light, sound, water, or electrical modality treatments such as ultrasound. Change linens, such as bedsheets and pillowcases. Arrange treatment supplies to keep them in order. Assist patients in dressing and undressing and putting on and removing supportive devices, such as braces, splints, and slings. Measure patient's range of joint motion, body parts, and vital signs to determine effects of treatments or to evaluate the patient's condition. Train patients to use orthopedic braces, prostheses, or supportive devices. Fit patients for orthopedic braces, prostheses, or supportive devices, adjusting fit as needed. Participate in patient care tasks, such as assisting with passing food trays, feeding residents, or bathing residents on bed rest. Administer traction to relieve neck and back pain, using intermittent and static traction equipment.

EYE OPENERS

Physical therapist aides may face keen competition from the large pool of qualified applicants.

- Annual earnings (average): $21,510
- Annual earnings (starting): $15,580
- Employed: 43,000
- Growth: 34.4%
- Annual job openings: 5,000

PREPARING FOR THE JOB

Education/training required: Short-term on-the-job training.

Programs: Physical therapist assistant training.

Knowledge/courses: Psychology; medicine and dentistry; therapy and counseling; customer and personal service; clerical practices; education and training; English language.

Licensure/certification: Not relevant.

WORKING CONDITIONS

Physical: Indoors; disease or infections; standing; walking and running; using hands on objects, tools, or controls; repetitive motions.

Work settings: Hospitals, therapists' offices, and other health-care facilities.

Other job characteristics: Need to be exact or accurate; errors have important consequences.

OTHER FACTS

O*NET code: 31-2022.00

GOE information: Interest area: 08. Health Science. Work group: 08.07. Medical Therapy.

Personality type: Social. Social occupations frequently involve working with, communicating with, and teaching people. These occupations often involve helping or providing service to others.

TOP SKILLS

- Social perceptiveness
- Service orientation
- Operation monitoring
- Equipment maintenance
- Time management
- Learning strategies

WHERE TO FIND OUT MORE

For information on employment opportunities, contact local employers or local offices of the state employment service.

video number 7

Veterinary Assistants and Laboratory Animal Caretakers

QUICK LOOK

Feed, water, and examine pets and other nonfarm animals for signs of illness, disease, or injury in laboratories and animal hospitals and clinics. May provide routine post-operative care, administer medication orally or topically, or prepare samples for laboratory examination under the supervision of veterinary or laboratory animal technologists or technicians, veterinarians, or scientists. Monitor animals recovering from surgery and notify veterinarians of any unusual changes or symptoms. Administer anesthetics during surgery and monitor the effects on animals. Clean, maintain, and sterilize laboratory and surgical instruments and equipment. Administer medication, immunizations, and blood plasma to animals as prescribed by veterinarians. Provide emergency first aid to sick or injured animals. Clean and maintain kennels, animal holding areas, examination and operating rooms, and animal loading/unloading facilities to control the spread of disease. Hold or restrain animals during veterinary procedures. Perform routine laboratory tests or diagnostic tests such as taking and developing X-rays. Fill medication prescriptions. Collect laboratory specimens such as blood, urine, and feces for testing. Examine animals to detect behavioral changes or clinical symptoms that could indicate illness or injury. Assist veterinarians in examining animals to determine the nature of illnesses or injuries.

Prepare surgical equipment and pass instruments and materials to veterinarians during surgical procedures. Perform enemas, catheterization, ear flushes, intravenous feedings, and gavages. Prepare feed for animals according to specific instructions such as diet lists and schedules. Exercise animals and provide them with companionship. Record information relating to animal genealogy, feeding schedules, appearance, behavior, and breeding. Educate and advise clients on animal health care, nutrition, and behavior problems. Perform hygiene-related duties such as clipping animals' claws and cleaning and polishing teeth. Prepare examination or treatment rooms by stocking them with appropriate supplies. Provide assistance with euthanasia of animals and disposal of corpses. Perform office reception duties such as scheduling appointments and helping customers. Dust, spray, or bathe animals to control insect pests. Write reports, maintain research information, and perform clerical duties. Perform accounting duties, including bookkeeping, billing customers for services, and maintaining inventories. Assist professional personnel with research projects in commercial, public health, or research laboratories.

PREPARING FOR THE JOB

Education/training required: Short-term on-the-job training.

Programs: Veterinary/animal health technology/technician and veterinary assistant training.

Knowledge/courses: Medicine and dentistry; biology; chemistry; clerical practices.

Licensure/certification: Certification available.

WORKING CONDITIONS

Physical: Indoors; disease or infections; minor burns, cuts, bites, or stings; standing; walking and running; using hands on objects, tools, or controls.

Work settings: Veterinarians' offices, kennels, farms, laboratories, or meat-processing plants.

Other job characteristics: Need to be exact or accurate; errors have important consequences; repeat same tasks.

OTHER FACTS

O*NET code: 31-9096.00

GOE information: Interest area: 08. Health Science. Work group: 08.05. Animal Care.

Personality type: Realistic. Realistic occupations frequently involve work activities that include practical, hands-on problems and solutions. They often deal with plants, animals, and real-world materials like wood, tools, and machinery. Many of the occupations require working outside and do not involve a lot of paperwork or working closely with others.

TOP SKILLS

- Science
- Operation monitoring
- Active listening
- Reading comprehension
- Instructing
- Equipment maintenance

WHERE TO FIND OUT MORE

For more information about careers with laboratory animals, contact

➤ American Association for Laboratory Animal Science, 9190 Crestwyn Hills Dr., Memphis, TN 38125-8538. Internet: www.aalas.org/index.aspx

➤ Laboratory Animal Management Association, 7500 Flying Cloud Dr. #900, Eden Prairie, MN 55344. Internet: www.lama-online.org/index.htm

video number 8

Ambulance Drivers and Attendants, Except Emergency Medical Technicians

QUICK LOOK

Drive ambulance or assist ambulance driver in transporting sick, injured, or convalescent persons. Assist in lifting patients. Remove and replace soiled linens and equipment to maintain sanitary conditions. Accompany and assist emergency medical technicians on calls. Place patients on stretchers and load stretchers into ambulances, usually with assistance from other attendants. Earn and maintain appropriate certifications. Replace supplies and disposable items on ambulances. Report facts concerning accidents or emergencies to hospital personnel or law enforcement officials. Administer first aid such as bandaging, splinting, and administering oxygen. Restrain or shackle violent patients.

── EYE OPENERS ──

This job requires a lot of social interaction, both face-to-face and on the phone.

- Annual earnings (average): $18,790
- Annual earnings (starting): $13,630
- Employed: 20,000
- Growth: 28.0%
- Annual job openings: 5,000

PREPARING FOR THE JOB

Education/training required: Moderate-term on-the-job training.

Programs: Emergency medical technology/technician training (EMT Paramedic).

Knowledge/courses: Transportation; psychology; medicine and dentistry; customer and personal service; telecommunications; public safety and security; law and government.

Licensure/certification: Driver's license, perhaps specialized, required in all states; certification available.

WORKING CONDITIONS

Physical: Outdoors; noisy; very hot or cold; disease or infections; sitting; using hands on objects, tools, or controls.

Work settings: Ambulances and reception areas of hospitals and other health-care facilities.

Other job characteristics: Need to be exact or accurate; errors have important consequences.

OTHER FACTS

O*NET code: 53-3011.00

GOE information: Interest area: 16. Transportation, Distribution, and Logistics. Work group: 16.06. Other Services Requiring Driving.

Personality type: Social. Social occupations frequently involve working with, communicating with, and teaching people. These occupations often involve helping or providing service to others.

WHERE TO FIND OUT MORE

For information on employment opportunities, contact local employers or local offices of the state employment service.

TOP SKILLS

- Equipment maintenance
- Operation monitoring
- Operation and control
- Repairing
- Technology design
- Service orientation

Moderate-Term
On-the-Job Training

Animal Trainers

QUICK LOOK

Conduct training programs to develop and maintain desired animal behaviors for competition, entertainment, obedience, security, riding, and service to people with disabilities. May train animals to carry pack loads or work as part of a pack team. Condition animals to respond to commands. Train animals according to prescribed standards for show or competition. Cue or signal animals during performances. Train and rehearse animals, according to scripts, for motion picture, television, film, stage, or circus performances. Organize and conduct animal shows. Observe animals' physical conditions to detect illness or unhealthy conditions requiring medical care. Administer prescribed medications to animals. Evaluate animals to determine their temperaments, abilities, and aptitude for training. Feed and exercise animals and provide other general care such as cleaning and maintaining holding and performance areas. Talk to and interact with animals in order to familiarize them to human voices and contact. Keep records documenting animal health, diet, and behavior. Advise animal owners regarding the purchase of specific animals. Train dogs in human-assistance or property protection duties. Train horses or other equines for riding, harness, show, racing, or other work, using knowledge of breed characteristics, training methods, performance standards, and the peculiarities of each animal.

EYE OPENERS

Most workers are trained on the job, but employers generally prefer to hire people who have some experience with animals.

- Annual earnings (average): $24,800
- Annual earnings (starting): $15,330
- Employed: 44,000
- Growth: 20.3%
- Annual job openings: 3,000

Use oral, spur, rein, and hand commands to condition horses to carry riders or to pull horse-drawn equipment. Instruct jockeys in handling specific horses during races. Place tack or harnesses on horses to accustom horses to the feel of equipment. Retrain horses to break bad habits, such as kicking, bolting, and resisting bridling and grooming. Arrange for mating of stallions and mares and assist mares during foaling.

PREPARING FOR THE JOB

Education/training required: Moderate-term on-the-job training.

Programs: Animal training; equestrian/equine studies.

Knowledge/courses: Sales and marketing; biology; customer and personal service; economics and accounting; communications and media; clerical practices; personnel and human resources.

Licensure/certification: Certification available.

WORKING CONDITIONS

Physical: Outdoors; noisy; standing; walking and running; using hands on objects, tools, or controls; repetitive motions.

Work settings: Pet stores, clients' homes, or places where animals perform, such as arenas or movie studios.

Other job characteristics: None significant.

OTHER FACTS

O*NET code: 39-2011.00

GOE information: Interest area: 08. Health Science. Work group: 08.05. Animal Care.

TOP SKILLS

- Management of financial resources
- Persuasion
- Instructing
- Service orientation
- Learning strategies
- Monitoring

Personality type: Social. Social occupations frequently involve working with, communicating with, and teaching people. These occupations often involve helping or providing service to others.

WHERE TO FIND OUT MORE

For information on employment opportunities, contact local employers or local offices of the state employment service.

Dental Assistants

QUICK LOOK

Assist dentists, prepare patients, set up equipment, and keep records. Sterilize and disinfect instruments, set up instrument trays, prepare materials, and help dentists during dental procedures. Expose dental diagnostic X-rays. Record treatment information in patient records. Take and record medical and dental histories and vital signs of patients. Provide postoperative instructions prescribed by a dentist. Assist dentists in management of medical and dental emergencies. Pour, trim, and polish study casts. Instruct patients in oral hygiene and plaque control programs. Make preliminary impressions for study casts and occlusal registrations for mounting study casts. Clean and polish removable appliances. Clean teeth, using dental instruments. Apply protective coating of fluoride to teeth. Fabricate temporary restorations and custom impressions from preliminary impressions. Schedule appointments, prepare bills, and receive payment for dental services. Complete insurance forms and maintain records, either manually or by using a computer.

EYE OPENERS

Most dental assistants learn their skills on the job, although an increasing number are trained in dental-assisting programs. Most of these programs take one year or less to complete.

- Annual earnings (average): $29,520
- Annual earnings (starting): $19,680
- Employed: 267,000
- Growth: 42.7%
- Annual job openings: 45,000

PREPARING FOR THE JOB

Education/training required: Moderate-term on-the-job training.

Programs: Dental assisting/assistant training.

Knowledge/courses: Medicine and dentistry; chemistry; clerical practices; customer and personal service; psychology; computers and electronics; public safety and security; mechanical devices.

Licensure/certification: Certification available; certification or licensure required in some states.

WORKING CONDITIONS

Physical: Indoors; contaminants; disease or infections; using hands on objects, tools, or controls; bending or twisting the body; repetitive motions.

Work settings: Dentists' offices.

Other job characteristics: Need to be exact or accurate; repeat same tasks.

OTHER FACTS

O*NET code: 31-9091.00

GOE information: Interest area: 08. Health Science. Work group: 08.03. Dentistry.

TOP SKILLS

- Equipment maintenance
- Social perceptiveness
- Operation and control
- Management of material resources
- Operation monitoring
- Equipment selection

Personality type: Social. Social occupations frequently involve working with, communicating with, and teaching people. These occupations often involve helping or providing service to others.

WHERE TO FIND OUT MORE

Information about career opportunities and accredited dental assistant programs is available from

➤ American Dental Association, Commission on Dental Accreditation, 211 E. Chicago Ave., Chicago, IL 60611. Internet: www.ada.org

For information on becoming a certified dental assistant and a list of state boards of dentistry, contact

➤ Dental Assisting National Board, Inc., 444 N. Michigan Ave., Suite 900, Chicago, IL 60611. Internet: www.danb.org

Moderate-Term On-the-Job Training

Medical Assistants

QUICK LOOK

Perform administrative and certain clinical duties under the direction of a physician. Administrative duties may include scheduling appointments, maintaining medical records, billing, and coding for insurance purposes. Clinical duties may include taking and recording vital signs and medical histories, preparing patients for examination, drawing blood, and administering medications as directed by a physician. Interview patients to obtain medical information and measure their vital signs, weight, and height. Show patients to examination rooms and prepare them for the physician. Record patients' medical history, vital statistics, and information such as test results in medical records. Prepare and administer medications as directed by a physician. Collect blood, tissue, or other laboratory specimens; log the specimens; and prepare them for testing. Explain treatment procedures, medications, diets, and physicians' instructions to patients. Help physicians examine and treat patients, handing them instruments and materials or performing such tasks as giving injections or removing sutures. Authorize drug refills and provide prescription information to pharmacies. Prepare treatment rooms for patient examinations, keeping the rooms neat and clean. Clean and sterilize instruments and dispose of contaminated supplies. Schedule appointments for patients. Change dressings on wounds. Greet and log in patients arriving at an office or clinic. Contact medical facilities or departments to schedule patients for tests or admission. Perform general office duties such as answering telephones, taking dictation, or completing insurance forms. Inventory and order medical, lab, or office supplies and equipment. Perform routine laboratory tests and sample analyses. Set up medical laboratory equipment. Keep financial records and perform other bookkeeping duties, such as handling credit and collections and mailing monthly statements to patients. Operate X-ray, electrocardiogram (EKG), and other equipment to administer routine diagnostic tests. Give physiotherapy treatments such as diathermy, galvanics, and hydrotherapy.

── EYE OPENERS ──

Some medical assistants are trained on the job, but many complete one- or two-year programs in vocational-technical high schools, postsecondary vocational schools, and community and junior colleges.

- Annual earnings (average): $25,350
- Annual earnings (starting): $18,330
- Employed: 387,000
- Growth: 52.1%
- Annual job openings: 93,000

PREPARING FOR THE JOB

Education/training required: Moderate-term on-the-job training.

Programs: Allied health and medical assisting services; anesthesiologist assistant training; chiropractic assistant/technician training; medical administrative/executive assistant and medical secretary training; medical insurance coding specialist/coder training; medical office assistant/specialist training; medical office management/administration; medical reception/receptionist training; medical/clinical assistant training; opthalmic technician/technologist training; optomeric technician/assistant training; orthoptics/orthoptist training.

Knowledge/courses: Medicine and dentistry; therapy and counseling; customer and personal service; clerical practices; psychology; English language; chemistry.

Licensure/certification: Certification available.

WORKING CONDITIONS

Physical: Indoors; disease or infections; standing; walking and running; using hands on objects, tools, or controls.

Work settings: Hospitals and other health-care facilities and physicians' offices.

Other job characteristics: Need to be exact or accurate; repeat same tasks.

TOP SKILLS

- Social perceptiveness
- Service orientation
- Instructing
- Operation monitoring
- Active listening
- Operation and control

OTHER FACTS

O*NET code: 31-9092.00

GOE information: Interest area: 08. Health Science. Work group: 08.02. Medicine and Surgery.

Personality type: Social. Social occupations frequently involve working with, communicating with, and teaching people. These occupations often involve helping or providing service to others.

WHERE TO FIND OUT MORE

Information about career opportunities and the Certified Medical Assistant (CMA) exam is available from

> ➤ American Association of Medical Assistants, 20 N. Wacker Dr., Suite 1575, Chicago, IL 60606. Internet: www.aama-ntl.org

Information about career opportunities and the Registered Medical Assistant (RMA) certification exam is available from

> ➤ American Medical Technologists, 10700 W. Higgins Rd., Rosemont, IL 60018. Internet: www.amt1.com

Ophthalmic Laboratory Technicians

QUICK LOOK

Cut, grind, and polish eyeglasses, contact lenses, or other precision optical elements. Assemble and mount lenses into frames or process other optical elements. Adjust lenses and frames to correct alignment. Mount, secure, and align finished lenses in frames or optical assemblies, using precision hand tools. Mount and secure lens blanks or optical lenses in holding tools or chucks of cutting, polishing, grinding, or coating machines. Shape lenses appropriately so that they can be inserted into frames. Assemble eyeglass frames and attach shields, nose pads, and temple pieces, using pliers, screwdrivers, and drills. Inspect lens blanks to detect flaws, verify smoothness of surface, and ensure thickness of coating on lenses. Clean finished lenses and eyeglasses, using cloths and solvents. Select lens blanks, molds, tools, and polishing or grinding wheels according to production specifications. Examine prescriptions, work orders, or broken or used eyeglasses to determine specifications for lenses, contact lenses, and other optical elements. Set dials and start machines to polish lenses or hold lenses against rotating wheels to polish them manually. Set up machines to polish, bevel, edge, and grind lenses, flats, blanks, and other precision optical elements. Repair broken parts, using precision hand tools and soldering irons. Position and adjust cutting tools to specified curvature, dimensions, and depth of cut. Inspect, weigh, and measure mounted or unmounted lenses after completion to verify alignment and conformance to specifications, using precision instruments. Remove lenses from molds and separate lenses in containers for further processing or storage. Lay out lenses and trace lens outlines on glass, using templates. Immerse eyeglass frames in solutions to harden, soften, or dye frames. Control equipment that coats lenses to alter their reflective qualities.

EYE OPENERS

Employers filling trainee jobs prefer applicants who are high school graduates. Courses in science, mathematics, and computers are valuable; manual dexterity and the ability to do precision work are essential.

- Annual earnings (average): $24,740
- Annual earnings (starting): $16,890
- Employed: 25,000
- Growth: 7.8%
- Annual job openings: 2,000

PREPARING FOR THE JOB

Education/training required: Moderate-term on-the-job training.

Programs: Ophthalmic laboratory technology/technician training.

Knowledge/courses: Computers and electronics; administration and management; mathematics.

Licensure/certification: Certification available.

WORKING CONDITIONS

Physical: Indoors; noisy; standing; walking and running; using hands on objects, tools, or controls; repetitive motions.

Work settings: Ophthalmic laboratories.

Other job characteristics: Need to be exact or accurate; pace determined by speed of equipment; repeat same tasks.

OTHER FACTS

O*NET code: 51-9083.00

GOE information: Interest area: 13. Manufacturing. Work group: 13.06. Production Precision Work.

Personality type: Realistic. Realistic occupations frequently involve work activities that include practical, hands-on problems and solutions. They often deal with plants, animals, and real-world materials like wood, tools, and machinery. Many of these occupations require working outside and do not involve a lot of paperwork or working closely with others.

TOP SKILLS

- Repairing
- Service orientation
- Operation monitoring
- Quality control analysis
- Instructing
- Management of material resources

WHERE TO FIND OUT MORE

For information on an accredited program in ophthalmic laboratory technology, contact

➤ Commission on Opticianry Accreditation, P.O. Box 4342, Chapel Hill, NC 27515. Internet: www.coaccreditation.com/

Pharmacy Technicians

QUICK LOOK

Prepare medications under the direction of a pharmacist. May measure, mix, count out, label, and record amounts and dosages of medications. Receive written prescription or refill requests and verify that the information is complete and accurate. Maintain proper storage and security conditions for drugs. Answer telephones, responding to questions or requests. Fill bottles with prescribed medications and type and affix labels. Assist customers by answering questions, locating items, or referring them to the pharmacist for medication information. Price and file prescriptions that have been filled. Clean and help maintain equipment and work areas and sterilize glassware according to prescribed methods. Establish and maintain patient profiles, including lists of medications taken by individual patients. Order, label, and count stock of medications, chemicals, and supplies and enter inventory data into a computer. Receive and store incoming supplies, verify quantities against invoices, and inform supervisors of stock needs and shortages. Transfer medication from vials to the appropriate number of sterile disposable syringes, using aseptic techniques. Under a pharmacist's supervision, add measured drugs or nutrients to intravenous solutions in sterile conditions to prepare intravenous (IV) packs. Supply and monitor robotic machines that dispense medicine into containers and label the containers. Prepare and process medical insurance claim forms and records. Mix pharmaceutical preparations according to written prescriptions. Operate cash registers to accept payment from customers. Compute charges for medication and equipment dispensed to hospital patients and enter data in a computer. Deliver medications and pharmaceutical supplies to patients, nursing stations, or surgery departments. Price stock and mark items for sale. Maintain and merchandise home health-care products and services.

━━ EYE OPENERS ━━

Job opportunities for pharmacy technicians are expected to be good for full-time and part-time work, especially for those with certification or previous work experience.

- Annual earnings (average): $24,390
- Annual earnings (starting): $17,100
- Employed: 258,000
- Growth: 28.6%
- Annual job openings: 35,000

PREPARING FOR THE JOB

Education/training required: Moderate-term on-the-job training.

Programs: Pharmacy technician/assistant training.

Knowledge/courses: Medicine and dentistry; chemistry; customer and personal service; mathematics; clerical practices; computers and electronics; law and government.

Licensure/certification: Certification available.

WORKING CONDITIONS

Physical: Indoors; standing; using hands on objects, tools, or controls; repetitive motions.

Work settings: Hospitals and retail pharmacies.

Other job characteristics: Need to be exact or accurate; repeat same tasks.

OTHER FACTS

O*NET code: 29-2052.00

GOE information: Interest area: 08. Health Science. Work group: 08.02. Medicine and Surgery.

Personality type: Conventional. Conventional occupations frequently involve following set procedures and routines. These occupations can include working with data and details more than with ideas. Usually there is a clear line of authority to follow.

TOP SKILLS

- Service orientation
- Active listening
- Instructing
- Mathematics
- Speaking
- Active learning

Moderate-Term On-the-Job Training

WHERE TO FIND OUT MORE

For information on the Certified Pharmacy Technician designation, contact

➤ Pharmacy Technician Certification Board, 1100 15th St. NW, Suite 730, Washington, DC 20005-1707. Internet: www.ptcb.org

For a list of accredited pharmacy technician training programs, contact

➤ American Society of Health-System Pharmacists, 7272 Wisconsin Ave., Bethesda, MD 20814. Internet: www.ashp.org

For pharmacy technician career information, contact

➤ National Pharmacy Technician Association, P.O. Box 683148, Houston, TX 77268. Internet: www.pharmacytechnician.org

Social and Human Service Assistants

QUICK LOOK

Assist professionals from a wide variety of fields, such as psychology, rehabilitation, or social work, to provide client services, as well as support for families. May assist clients in identifying and obtaining available benefits and social and community services. May assist social workers with developing, organizing, and conducting programs to prevent and resolve problems relevant to substance abuse, human relationships, rehabilitation, or adult day care. Provide information and refer individuals to public or private agencies or community services for assistance. Keep records and prepare reports for owners or management concerning visits with clients. Visit individuals in homes or attend group meetings to provide information on agency services, requirements, and procedures. Advise clients regarding food stamps, child care, food, money management, sanitation, or housekeeping. Submit reports and review reports or problems with a superior. Oversee day-to-day group activities of residents in an institution. Interview individuals and family members to compile information on social, educational, criminal, institutional, or drug history. Meet with youth groups to acquaint them with consequences of delinquent acts. Transport and accompany clients to shopping areas or to appointments, using an automobile. Explain rules established by owners or management, such as sanitation and maintenance requirements and parking regulations. Observe and discuss meal preparation and suggest alternative methods of food preparation. Demonstrate use and care of equipment for tenant use. Consult with supervisor concerning programs for individual families. Monitor free, supplementary meal programs to ensure cleanliness of the facility and that eligibility guidelines are met for persons receiving meals. Observe clients' food selections and recommend alternative economical and nutritional food choices. Inform tenants of facilities such as laundries and playgrounds. Care for children in client's home during client's appointments. Assist in locating housing for displaced individuals. Assist clients with preparation of forms, such as tax or rent forms. Assist in planning of food budget, using charts and sample budgets.

— EYE OPENERS —

Although a bachelor's degree usually is not required for this job, employers increasingly seek individuals with relevant work experience or education beyond high school.

- Annual earnings (average): $25,030
- Annual earnings (starting): $15,830
- Employed: 352,000
- Growth: 29.7%
- Annual job openings: 61,000

PREPARING FOR THE JOB

Education/training required: Moderate-term on-the-job training.

Programs: Mental and social health services and allied professions.

Knowledge/courses: Therapy and counseling; psychology; philosophy and theology; sociology and anthropology; clerical practices; customer and personal service; education and training; law and government.

Licensure/certification: Certification available.

WORKING CONDITIONS

Physical: Indoors; noisy; sitting.

Work settings: Offices, clinics, hospitals, group homes, shelters, sheltered workshops, and day programs.

Other job characteristics: Need to be exact or accurate; repeat same tasks.

OTHER FACTS

O*NET code: 21-1093.00

GOE information: Interest area: 10. Human Service. Work group: 10.01. Counseling and Social Work.

TOP SKILLS

- Social perceptiveness
- Management of financial resources
- Service orientation
- Speaking
- Judgment and decision making
- Active listening

Personality type: Social. Social occupations frequently involve working with, communicating with, and teaching people. These occupations often involve helping or providing service to others.

WHERE TO FIND OUT MORE

Information on academic programs in human services may be found in most directories of two-year and four-year colleges, available at libraries or career counseling centers.

For information on programs and careers in human services, contact

➤ National Organization for Human Services, 90 Madison St., Suite 206, Denver, CO 80206-5418. Internet: www.nationalhumanservices.org

➤ Council for Standards in Human Service Education, 1050 Larrabee Ave., Suite 104, Bellingham, WA 98225-7367. Internet: www.cshse.org

Information on job openings may be available from state employment service offices or directly from city, county, or state departments of health, mental health and mental retardation, and human resources.

Dental Laboratory Technicians

QUICK LOOK

Construct and repair full or partial dentures or dental appliances. Read prescriptions or specifications and examine models and impressions to determine the design of dental products to be constructed. Fabricate, alter, and repair dental devices such as dentures, crowns, bridges, inlays, and appliances for straightening teeth. Place tooth models on apparatus that mimics bite and movement of a patient's jaw to evaluate functionality of model. Test appliances for conformance to specifications and accuracy of occlusion, using articulators and micrometers. Melt metals or mix plaster, porcelain, or acrylic pastes and pour materials into molds or over frameworks to form dental prostheses or apparatus. Prepare metal surfaces for bonding with porcelain to create artificial teeth, using small hand tools. Remove excess metal or porcelain and polish surfaces of prostheses or frameworks, using polishing machines. Create a model of a patient's mouth by pouring plaster into a dental impression and allowing the plaster to set. Load newly constructed teeth into porcelain furnaces to bake the porcelain onto the metal framework. Build and shape wax teeth, using small hand instruments and information from observations or dentists' specifications. Apply porcelain paste or wax over prosthesis frameworks or setups, using brushes and spatulas. Fill chipped or low spots in surfaces of devices, using acrylic resins. Prepare wax bite-blocks and impression trays for use. Mold wax over denture setups to form the full contours of artificial gums. Train and supervise other dental technicians or dental laboratory bench workers. Rebuild or replace linings, wire sections, and missing teeth to repair dentures. Shape and solder wire and metal frames or bands for dental products, using soldering irons and hand tools.

— EYE OPENERS —

Unlike most health-care workers, dental laboratory technicians use artistic ability in their work.

- Annual earnings (average): $32,240
- Annual earnings (starting): $18,760
- Employed: 50,000
- Growth: 7.6%
- Annual job openings: 3,000

PREPARING FOR THE JOB

Education/training required: Long-term on-the-job training.

Programs: Dental laboratory technology/technician training.

Knowledge/courses: Medicine and dentistry; design; production and processing; engineering and technology; mechanical devices; chemistry; education and training; administration and management.

Licensure/certification: Certification available.

WORKING CONDITIONS

Physical: Indoors; noisy; contaminants; sitting; using hands on objects, tools, or controls; repetitive motions.

Work settings: Dental laboratories.

Other job characteristics: Need to be exact or accurate; repeat same tasks.

OTHER FACTS

O*NET code: 51-9081.00

GOE information: Interest area: 13. Manufacturing. Work group: 13.06. Production Precision Work.

Personality type: Realistic. Realistic occupations frequently involve work activities that include practical, hands-on problems and solutions. They often deal with plants, animals, and real-world materials like wood, tools, and machinery. Many of the occupations require working outside and do not involve a lot of paperwork or working closely with others.

── TOP SKILLS ──

- Equipment maintenance
- Equipment selection
- Management of material resources
- Repairing
- Quality control analysis
- Operation monitoring

WHERE TO FIND OUT MORE

For a list of accredited programs in dental laboratory technology, contact

➤ American Dental Association, Commission on Dental Accreditation, 211 E. Chicago Ave., Chicago, IL 60611. Internet: www.ada.org

For information about requirements for certification for dental laboratory technicians, contact

➤ National Board for Certification in Dental Laboratory Technology, 325 John Knox Rd., #L103, Tallahassee, FL 32303. Internet: www.nbccert.org

For information on career opportunities in commercial dental laboratories, contact

➤ National Association of Dental Laboratories, 325 John Knox Rd., #L103, Tallahassee, FL 32303. Internet: www.nadl.org

Long-Term On-the-Job Training

Medical Appliance Technicians

QUICK LOOK

Construct, fit, maintain, or repair medical supportive devices, such as braces, artificial limbs and joints, arch supports, and other surgical and medical appliances. Fit appliances onto patients and make any necessary adjustments. Make orthotic/prosthetic devices using materials such as thermoplastic and thermosetting materials, metal alloys and leather, and hand and power tools. Read prescriptions or specifications to determine the type of product or device to be fabricated and the materials and tools that will be required. Repair, modify, and maintain medical supportive devices according to specifications. Instruct patients in use of prosthetic or orthotic devices. Take patients' body or limb measurements for use in device construction. Construct or receive casts or impressions of patients' torsos or limbs for use as cutting and fabrication patterns. Bend, form, and shape fabric or material so that it conforms to prescribed contours needed to fabricate structural components. Drill and tap holes for rivets and glue, weld, bolt, and rivet parts together to form prosthetic or orthotic devices. Lay out and mark dimensions of parts, using templates and precision measuring instruments. Test medical supportive devices for proper alignment, movement, and biomechanical stability, using meters and alignment fixtures. Cover or pad metal or plastic structures and devices, using coverings such as rubber, leather, felt, plastic, or fiberglass. Polish artificial limbs, braces, and supports, using grinding and buffing wheels. Service and repair machinery used in the fabrication of appliances. Mix pigments to match patients' skin coloring, according to formulas, and apply mixtures to orthotic or prosthetic devices.

— EYE OPENERS —

Formal training for this occupation is available. Currently, four programs are actively accredited by the National Commission on Orthotic and Prosthetic Education (NCOPE).

- Annual earnings (average): $29,080
- Annual earnings (starting): $17,470
- Employed: 11,000
- Growth: 13.2%
- Annual job openings: 1,000

PREPARING FOR THE JOB

Education/training required: Long-term on-the-job training.

Programs: Assistive/augmentative technology and rehabiliation engineering; orthotist/prosthetist training.

Knowledge/courses: Production and processing; design; mechanical devices; medicine and dentistry; customer and personal service; engineering and technology; therapy and counseling; psychology.

Licensure/certification: Certification available.

WORKING CONDITIONS

Physical: Indoors; noisy; contaminants; disease or infections; hazardous equipment; using hands on objects, tools, or controls.

Work settings: Medical appliance fabrication laboratories, hospitals, and other health-care facilities.

Other job characteristics: Need to be exact or accurate.

TOP SKILLS

- Technology design
- Repairing
- Installation
- Quality control analysis
- Active learning
- Science

OTHER FACTS

O*NET code: 51-9082.00

GOE information: Interest area: 13. Manufacturing. Work group: 13.06. Production Precision Work.

Personality type: Realistic. Realistic occupations frequently involve work activities that include practical, hands-on problems and solutions. They often deal with plants, animals, and real-world materials like wood, tools, and machinery. Many of these occupations require working outside and do not involve a lot of paperwork or working closely with others.

WHERE TO FIND OUT MORE

For information on careers in medical appliances, contact

➤ American Academy of Orthotists and Prosthetists, 526 King St., Suite 201, Alexandria, VA 22314. Internet: www.opcareers.org

For a list of accredited programs in medical applicances, contact

➤ National Commission on Orthotic and Prosthetic Education, 330 John Carlyle St., Suite 200, Alexandria, VA 22314. Internet: www.ncope.org

To read an interview with someone working in this field, visit the following site on the Internet:

➤ National Institutes of Health Office of Science Education: science.education.nih.gov/LifeWorks.nsf/Interviews/Ron+Dickey

Opticians, Dispensing

QUICK LOOK

Design, measure, fit, and adapt lenses and frames for clients according to written optical prescriptions or specifications. Assist clients with selecting frames. Measure customers for their size of eyeglasses. Prepare work orders containing instructions for grinding and mounting lenses in frames. Verify exactness of finished lens spectacles. Adjust frame and lens position to fit clients. May shape or reshape frames. Measure clients' bridge and eye size, temple length, vertex distance, pupillary distance, and optical centers of eyes, using measuring devices. Verify that finished lenses are ground to specifications. Prepare instructions for optical laboratories that give details for grinding lenses and fabricating eyeglasses. Help clients in choosing frames according to style and color and ensure that frames are coordinated with facial and eye measurements and optical prescriptions. Maintain records of customer prescriptions, work orders, and payments. Perform administrative duties such as tracking inventory and sales, submitting patient insurance information, and performing simple bookkeeping. Recommend specific lenses, lens coatings, and frames to suit client needs. Sell goods such as contact lenses, spectacles, sunglasses, and other goods related to eyes in general. Heat, shape, or bend plastic or metal frames to adjust eyeglasses to fit clients, using pliers and hands. Evaluate prescriptions in conjunction with clients' vocational and avocational visual requirements. Instruct clients in how to wear and care for eyeglasses. Determine clients' current lens prescriptions, when necessary, using lensometers or lens analyzers and clients' eyeglasses. Show customers how to insert, remove, and care for their contact lenses. Repair damaged frames. Obtain a customer's previous record or verify a prescription with the examining optometrist or ophthalmologist. Arrange and maintain displays of optical merchandise. Fabricate lenses to meet prescription specifications. Grind lens edges or apply coatings to lenses. Assemble eyeglasses by cutting and edging lenses and fitting the lenses into frames. Supervise the training of student opticians.

— EYE OPENERS —

About 20 states require a license for dispensing opticians.

- Annual earnings (average): $29,000
- Annual earnings (starting): $18,490
- Employed: 66,000
- Growth: 13.6%
- Annual job openings: 6,000

PREPARING FOR THE JOB

Education/training required: Long-term on-the-job training.

Programs: Opticianry/ophthalmic dispensing optician training.

Knowledge/courses: Sales and marketing; customer and personal service; production and processing; clerical practices; economics and accounting; psychology; administration and management; personnel and human resources.

Licensure/certification: Certification available; licensure required in some states.

WORKING CONDITIONS

Physical: Indoors; standing; using hands on objects, tools, or controls.

Work settings: Medical offices or stores.

Other job characteristics: Need to be exact or accurate; repeat same tasks.

OTHER FACTS

O*NET code: 29-2081.00

GOE information: Interest area: 08. Health Science. Work group: 08.06. Medical Technology.

Personality type: Enterprising. Enterprising occupations frequently involve starting up and carrying out projects. These occupations can involve leading people and making many decisions. They sometimes require risk taking and often deal with business.

TOP SKILLS

- Persuasion
- Service orientation
- Technology design
- Speaking
- Equipment selection
- Mathematics

WHERE TO FIND OUT MORE

For general information about opticians and a list of home-study programs, seminars, and review materials, contact

➤ National Academy of Opticianry, 8401 Corporate Dr., Suite 605, Landover, MD 20785. Telephone (toll-free): 800-229-4828. Internet: www.nao.org

For a list of accredited programs in opticianry, contact

➤ Commission on Opticianry Accreditation, P.O. Box 4342, Chapel Hill, NC 27515. Internet: www.coaccreditation.com/

QUICK LOOK

Direct activities such as autopsies, pathological and toxicological analyses, and inquests relating to the investigation of deaths occurring within a legal jurisdiction to determine cause of death or to fix responsibility for accidental, violent, or unexplained deaths. Perform medicolegal examinations and autopsies, conducting preliminary examinations of the body in order to identify victims, to locate signs of trauma, and to identify factors that would indicate time of death. Inquire into the cause, manner, and circumstances of human deaths and establish the identities of deceased persons. Direct activities of workers who conduct autopsies, perform pathological and toxicological analyses, and prepare documents for permanent records. Complete death certificates, including the assignment of a cause and manner of death. Observe and record the positions and conditions of bodies and of related evidence. Collect and document any pertinent medical history information. Observe, record, and preserve any objects or personal property related to deaths, including objects such as medication containers and suicide notes. Complete reports and forms required to finalize cases. Remove or supervise removal of bodies from death scenes, using the proper equipment and supplies, and arrange for transportation to morgues. Testify at inquests, hearings, and court trials. Interview persons present at death scenes to obtain information useful in determining the manner of death. Provide information concerning the circumstances of a person's death to relatives of the deceased. Locate and document information regarding the next of kin, including their relationship to the deceased and the status of notification attempts. Confer with officials of public health and law enforcement agencies in order to coordinate interdepartmental activities. Inventory personal effects, such as jewelry or wallets, that are recovered from bodies. Coordinate the release of personal effects to authorized persons and facilitate the disposition of unclaimed corpses and personal effects. Arrange for the next of kin to be notified of deaths. Record the disposition of minor children, as well as details of arrangements made for their care. Collect wills, burial instructions, and other documentation needed for investigations and for handling of the remains. Witness and certify deaths that are the result of a judicial order.

EYE OPENERS

Coroners usually are elected and may not need to be physicians. In contrast, medical examiners usually are appointed and usually need to be physicians.

- Annual earnings (average): $49,360
- Annual earnings (starting): $30,570
- Employed: 177,000
- Growth: 11.6%
- Annual job openings: 17,000

Our sources did not provide separate job openings data for this occupation. The figures for employment and job openings listed here are shared with environmental compliance inspectors, equal opportunity representatives and officers, government property inspectors and investigators, and licensing examiners and inspectors.

PREPARING FOR THE JOB

Education/training required: Work experience in a related occupation.

Programs: Public administration.

Knowledge/courses: Medicine and dentistry; biology; psychology; therapy and counseling; chemistry; law and government; sociology and anthropology; personnel and human resources.

Licensure/certification: Certification available.

WORKING CONDITIONS

Physical: More often indoors than outdoors; contaminants; disease or infections; hazardous equipment; using hands on objects, tools, or controls.

Work settings: Offices, medical examination rooms, crime scenes, and courtrooms.

Other job characteristics: Need to be exact or accurate; errors have important consequences.

TOP SKILLS

- Science
- Management of financial resources
- Management of personnel resources
- Reading comprehension
- Critical thinking
- Speaking

OTHER FACTS

O*NET code: 13-1041.06

GOE information: Interest area: 08. Health Science. Work group: 08.01. Managerial Work in Medical and Health Services.

Personality type: Investigative. Investigative occupations frequently involve working with ideas and require an extensive amount of thinking. These occupations can involve searching for facts and figuring out problems.

WHERE TO FIND OUT MORE

For more information about coroners and medical examiners, contact

➤ National Association of Medical Examiners, 430 Pryor St. SW Atlanta, GA 30312. Internet: thename.org

Work Experience in a Related Occupation

video number **19**

Emergency Medical Technicians and Paramedics

QUICK LOOK

Assess injuries, administer emergency medical care, and extricate trapped individuals. Transport injured or sick persons to medical facilities. Administer first-aid treatment and life-support care to sick or injured persons in prehospital setting. Operate equipment such as electrocardiograms (EKGs), external defibrillators, and bag-valve mask resuscitators in advanced life-support environments. Assess nature and extent of illness or injury to establish and prioritize medical procedures. Maintain vehicles and medical and communication equipment and replenish first-aid equipment and supplies. Observe, record, and report to a physician the patient's condition or injury, the treatment provided, and reactions to drugs and treatment. Perform emergency diagnostic and treatment procedures, such as stomach suction, airway management, or heart monitoring, during ambulance ride. Administer drugs, orally or by injection, and perform intravenous procedures under a physician's direction. Comfort and reassure patients. Coordinate work with other emergency medical team members and police and fire department personnel. Communicate with dispatchers and treatment center personnel to provide information about the situation, to arrange for the reception of victims, and to receive instructions for further treatment. Immobilize patient for placement on stretcher and ambulance transport, using a backboard or another spinal immobilization device. Decontaminate ambulance interior following the treatment of a patient with an infectious disease and report the case to proper authorities. Drive mobile intensive care unit to specified location, following instructions from emergency medical dispatcher. Coordinate with treatment center personnel to obtain patients' vital statistics and medical history, to determine the circumstances of the emergency, and to administer emergency treatment.

— EYE OPENERS —

Emergency medical technicians and paramedics need formal training and certification, but requirements vary by state.

- Annual earnings (average): $26,080
- Annual earnings (starting): $16,620
- Employed: 192,000
- Growth: 27.3%
- Annual job openings: 21,000

PREPARING FOR THE JOB

Education/training required: Postsecondary vocational training.

Programs: Emergency care attendant training (EMT ambulance); emergency medical technology/technician training (EMT paramedic).

Knowledge/courses: Medicine and dentistry; therapy and counseling; customer and personal service; chemistry; psychology; biology; public safety and security; transportation.

Licensure/certification: Certification available and required in some states.

WORKING CONDITIONS

Physical: Outdoors; noisy; very bright or dim lighting; contaminants; cramped work space; awkward positions; disease or infections.

Work settings: Both indoors and outdoors in all types of weather, wherever people need emergency help; ambulances and hospitals.

Other job characteristics: Errors have important consequences; need to be exact or accurate; repeat same tasks.

TOP SKILLS

- Equipment maintenance
- Operation monitoring
- Service orientation
- Social perceptiveness
- Operation and control
- Coordination

OTHER FACTS

O*NET code: 29-2041.00

GOE information: Interest area: 12. Law and Public Safety. Work group: 12.06. Emergency Responding.

Personality type: Social. Social occupations frequently involve working with, communicating with, and teaching people. These occupations often involve helping or providing service to others.

WHERE TO FIND OUT MORE

General information about emergency medical technicians and paramedics is available from

> ➤ National Association of Emergency Medical Technicians, P.O. Box 1400, Clinton, MS 39060-1400. Internet: www.naemt.org

> ➤ National Registry of Emergency Medical Technicians, Rocco V. Morando Building, 6610 Busch Blvd., P.O. Box 29233, Columbus, OH 43229. Internet: www.nremt.org

Fitness Trainers and Aerobics Instructors

QUICK LOOK

Instruct or coach groups or individuals in exercise activities and the fundamentals of sports. Demonstrate techniques and methods of participation. Observe participants and inform them of corrective measures necessary to improve their skills. Explain and enforce safety rules and regulations governing sports, recreational activities, and the use of exercise equipment. Offer alternatives during classes to accommodate different levels of fitness. Plan routines, choose appropriate music, and choose different movements for each set of muscles, depending on participants' capabilities and limitations. Teach proper breathing techniques used during physical exertion. Teach and demonstrate use of gymnastic and training equipment such as trampolines and weights. Instruct participants in maintaining exertion levels to maximize benefits from exercise routines. Maintain fitness equipment. Conduct therapeutic, recreational, or athletic activities. Monitor participants' progress and adapt programs as needed. Evaluate individuals' abilities, needs, and physical conditions and develop suitable training programs to meet any special requirements. Plan physical education programs to promote development of participants' physical attributes and social skills. Provide students with information and resources regarding nutrition, weight control, and lifestyle issues. Administer emergency first aid, wrap injuries, treat minor chronic disabilities, or refer injured persons to physicians. Advise clients about proper clothing and shoes for exercise. Wrap ankles, fingers, wrists, or other body parts with synthetic skin, gauze, or adhesive tape to support muscles and ligaments. Teach individual and team sports to participants through instruction and demonstration, utilizing knowledge of sports techniques and of participants' physical capabilities. Promote health clubs through membership sales and record member information. Organize, lead, and referee indoor and outdoor games such as volleyball, baseball, and basketball. Maintain equipment inventories and select, store, or issue equipment as needed. Organize and conduct competitions and tournaments. Advise participants in use of heat or ultraviolet treatments and hot baths. Massage body parts to relieve soreness, strains, and bruises.

EYE OPENERS

Many group fitness and personal training jobs are part-time, but many workers increase their hours by working at several different facilities or at clients' homes.

- Annual earnings (average): $25,840
- Annual earnings (starting): $14,540
- Employed: 205,000
- Growth: 27.1%
- Annual job openings: 50,000

Preparing for the Job

Education/training required: Postsecondary vocational training.

Programs: Health and physical education; physical education teaching and coaching; sport and fitness administration/management.

Knowledge/courses: Customer and personal service; psychology; education and training; sociology and anthropology; sales and marketing; personnel and human resources.

Licensure/certification: Certification available.

Working Conditions

Physical: Indoors; standing; walking and running; repetitive motions.

Work settings: Fitness centers and health clubs.

Other job characteristics: None significant.

Other Facts

O*NET code: 39-9031.00

GOE information: Interest area: 05. Education and Training. Work group: 05.06. Counseling, Health, and Fitness Education.

Personality type: Social. Social occupations frequently involve working with, communicating with, and teaching people. These occupations often involve helping or providing service to others.

TOP SKILLS

- Instructing
- Equipment selection
- Monitoring
- Service orientation
- Coordination
- Social perceptiveness

Where to Find Out More

To read more information about fitness careers and certifications, contact

➤ IDEA Health & Fitness Association, 10455 Pacific Center Ct., San Diego, CA 92121-4339. Internet: www.ideafit.com

➤ American Council on Exercise, 4851 Paramount Dr., San Diego, CA 92123. Internet: www.acefitness.org

➤ American College of Sports Medicine, P.O. Box 1440, Indianapolis, IN 46206-1440. Internet: www.acsm.org

➤ National Academy of Sports Medicine, 26632 Agoura Rd., Calabasas, CA 91032. Internet: www.nasm.org

➤ National Strength and Conditioning Association Certification Commission, 3333 Landmark Cirle, Lincoln, NE 68504. Internet: www.nsca-cc.org

QUICK LOOK

Care for ill, injured, convalescent, or disabled people in hospitals, nursing homes, clinics, private homes, group homes, and similar institutions. May work under the supervision of a registered nurse. Observe patients, charting and reporting changes in patients' conditions, such as adverse reactions to medication or treatment, and taking any necessary action. Administer prescribed medications or start intravenous fluids and note times and amounts on patients' charts. Answer patients' calls and determine how to assist them. Measure and record patients' vital signs, such as height, weight, temperature, blood pressure, pulse, and respiration. Provide basic patient care and treatments, such as taking temperatures or blood pressures, dressing wounds, treating bedsores, giving enemas or douches, rubbing with alcohol, massaging, or performing catheterizations. Help patients with bathing, dressing, maintaining personal hygiene, moving in bed, or standing and walking. Supervise nurses' aides and assistants. Work as part of a health-care team to assess patient needs, plan and modify care, and implement interventions. Record food and fluid intake and output. Evaluate nursing intervention outcomes, conferring with other health-care team members as necessary. Assemble and use equipment such as catheters, tracheotomy tubes, and oxygen suppliers. Collect samples such as blood, urine, and sputum from patients and perform routine laboratory tests on samples. Prepare patients for examinations, tests, or treatments and explain procedures. Prepare food trays and examine them for conformance to a prescribed diet. Apply compresses, ice bags, and hot water bottles. Clean rooms and make beds. Inventory and requisition supplies and instruments. Provide medical treatment and personal care, such as cooking, keeping rooms orderly, seeing that patients are comfortable and in good spirits, and instructing family members in simple nursing tasks, to patients in private home settings. Sterilize equipment and supplies, using germicides, sterilizer, or autoclave. Assist in delivery, care, and feeding of infants. Wash and dress bodies of deceased persons. Make appointments, keep records, and perform other clerical duties in doctors' offices and clinics. Set up equipment and prepare medical treatment rooms.

EYE OPENERS

Training that lasts about one year is available in approximately 1,200 state-approved programs, which are mostly in vocational or technical schools.

- Annual earnings (average): $35,230
- Annual earnings (starting): $25,340
- Employed: 726,000
- Growth: 17.1%
- Annual job openings: 84,000

PREPARING FOR THE JOB

Education/training required: Postsecondary vocational training.

Programs: Licensed practical/vocational nurse training (LPN, LVN, Cert, Dipl, AAS).

Knowledge/courses: Psychology; therapy and counseling; medicine and dentistry; customer and personal service; philosophy and theology; sociology and anthropology; biology; education and training.

Licensure/certification: Licensure required.

WORKING CONDITIONS

Physical: Indoors; disease or infections; standing; walking and running.

Work settings: Hospitals, doctors' offices, and other health-care facilities.

Other job characteristics: Need to be exact or accurate; errors have important consequences; repeat same tasks.

OTHER FACTS

O*NET code: 29-2061.00

GOE information: Interest area: 08. Health Science. Work group: 08.08. Patient Care and Assistance.

Personality type: Social. Social occupations frequently involve working with, communicating with, and teaching people. These occupations often involve helping or providing service to others.

TOP SKILLS

- Science
- Operation monitoring
- Service orientation
- Judgment and decision making
- Active listening
- Management of personnel resources

WHERE TO FIND OUT MORE

For information about practical nursing, contact any of the following organizations:

➤ National Association for Practical Nurse Education & Service, Inc., 1940 Duke St., Suite 200, Alexandria, VA 22314. Internet: www.napnes.org

➤ National League for Nursing, 61 Broadway, 33rd Floor, New York, NY 10006. Internet: www.nln.org

➤ National Federation of Licensed Practical Nurses, Inc., 605 Poole Dr., Garner, NC 27529. Internet: www.nflpn.org

Massage Therapists

QUICK LOOK

Massage customers for hygienic or remedial purposes. Confer with clients about their medical histories and any problems with stress or pain to determine whether massage would be helpful. Apply finger and hand pressure to specific points of the body. Massage and knead the muscles and soft tissues of the human body to provide courses of treatment for medical conditions and injuries or wellness maintenance. Maintain treatment records. Provide clients with guidance and information about techniques for postural improvement and stretching, strengthening, relaxation, and rehabilitative exercises. Assess clients' soft tissue condition, joint quality and function, muscle strength, and range of motion. Develop and propose client treatment plans that specify which types of massage are to be used. Refer clients to other types of therapists when necessary. Use complementary aids, such as infrared lamps, wet compresses, ice, and whirlpool baths, to promote clients' recovery, relaxation, and well-being. Treat clients in own offices or travel to clients' offices and homes. Consult with other healthcare professionals such as physiotherapists, chiropractors, physicians, and psychologists to develop treatment plans for clients. Prepare and blend oils and apply the blends to clients' skin.

— EYE OPENERS —

Many states require formal training and a national certification in order to practice massage therapy.

- Annual earnings (average): $32,890
- Annual earnings (starting): $15,000
- Employed: 97,000
- Growth: 23.6%
- Annual job openings: 12,000

PREPARING FOR THE JOB

Education/training required: Postsecondary vocational training.

Programs: Asian bodywork therapy; massage therapy/therapeutic massage; somatic bodywork and related therapeutic services.

Knowledge/courses: Therapy and counseling; psychology; sales and marketing; medicine and dentistry; chemistry; English language; customer and personal service.

Licensure/certification: Certification available; certification or licensure required in some states.

WORKING CONDITIONS

Physical: Indoors; standing; using hands on objects, tools, or controls; repetitive motions.

Work settings: Private offices, studios, hospitals, nursing homes, fitness centers, sports medicine facilities, airports, shopping malls, and clients' homes or offices.

Other job characteristics: Need to be exact or accurate; repeat same tasks.

— **TOP SKILLS** —

- Service orientation
- Active listening

OTHER FACTS

O*NET code: 31-9011.00

GOE information: Interest area: 08. Health Science. Work group: 08.07. Medical Therapy.

Personality type: No data available.

WHERE TO FIND OUT MORE

General information on becoming a massage therapist is available from state regulatory boards. For more information on becoming a massage therapist, contact the following organizations:

➤ Associated Bodywork & Massage Professionals, 1271 Sugarbush Dr., Evergreen, CO 80439. Internet: www.abmp.com

➤ American Massage Therapy Association, 500 Davis St., Suite 900, Evanston, IL 60201. Internet: www.amtamassage.org

Medical Secretaries

QUICK LOOK

Perform secretarial duties utilizing specific knowledge of medical terminology and hospital, clinic, or laboratory procedures. Duties include scheduling appointments, billing patients, and compiling and recording medical charts, reports, and correspondence. Schedule and confirm patient diagnostic appointments, surgeries, and medical consultations. Answer telephones and direct calls to appropriate staff. Receive and route messages and documents such as laboratory results to appropriate staff. Greet visitors, ascertain purpose of visit, and direct them to appropriate staff. Interview patients to complete documents, case histories, and forms such as intake and insurance forms. Maintain medical records, technical library, and correspondence files. Operate office equipment such as voice mail messaging systems and use word-processing, spreadsheet, and other software applications to prepare reports, invoices, financial statements, letters, case histories, and medical records. Transmit correspondence and medical records by mail, e-mail, or fax. Perform various clerical and administrative functions, such as ordering and maintaining an inventory of supplies. Arrange hospital admissions for patients. Transcribe recorded messages and practitioners' diagnoses and recommendations into patients' medical records. Perform bookkeeping duties, such as handling credits and collections, preparing and sending financial statements and bills, and keeping financial records. Complete insurance and other claim forms. Prepare correspondence and assist physicians or medical scientists with preparation of reports, speeches, articles, and conference proceedings.

EYE OPENERS

Qualified secretaries who broaden their knowledge of a company's operations and enhance their skills may be promoted to other positions such as senior or executive secretary, clerical supervisor, or office manager.

- Annual earnings (average): $27,320
- Annual earnings (starting): $19,190
- Employed: 373,000
- Growth: 17.0%
- Annual job openings: 55,000

PREPARING FOR THE JOB

Education/training required: Postsecondary vocational training.

Programs: Medical administrative/executive assistant and medical secretary training; medical insurance specialist/medical biller training; medical office assistant/specialist training.

Knowledge/courses: Telecommunications; clerical practices; customer and personal service; communications and media; computers and electronics; English language; transportation; education and training.

Licensure/certification: Certification available.

WORKING CONDITIONS

Physical: Noisy; disease or infections; sitting; using hands on objects, tools, or controls.

Work settings: Offices in hospitals, other health-care facilities, and doctors' practices.

Other Job Characteristics: Need to be exact or accurate; errors have important consequences; repeat same tasks.

TOP SKILLS

- Social perceptiveness
- Writing
- Management of material resources
- Active listening
- Reading comprehension
- Speaking

OTHER FACTS

O*NET code: 43-6013.00

GOE information: Interest area: 04. Business and Administration. Work group: 04.04. Secretarial Support.

Personality type: Conventional. Conventional occupations frequently involve following set procedures and routines. These occupations can include working with data and details more than with ideas. Usually there is a clear line of authority to follow.

WHERE TO FIND OUT MORE

For career information, contact

➤ International Association of Administrative Professionals, 10502 NW Ambassador Dr., P.O. Box 20404, Kansas City, MO 64195-0404. Internet: www.iaap-hq.org/

Medical Transcriptionists

QUICK LOOK

Use transcribing machines with headset and foot pedal to listen to recordings by physicians and other health-care professionals dictating a variety of medical reports. Transcribe dictated reports and translate medical jargon and abbreviations into their expanded forms. Edit reports as necessary and return them in either printed or electronic form to the dictator for review and signature or correction. Transcribe dictation for medical reports such as patient histories, physical examinations, diagnostic imaging studies, emergency room visits, operations, chart reviews, consultation, or discharge summaries. Review and edit transcribed reports or dictated material for spelling, grammar, clarity, consistency, and proper medical terminology. Distinguish between homonyms and recognize inconsistencies and mistakes in medical terms, referring to dictionaries; drug references; and other sources on anatomy, physiology, and medicine. Return dictated reports in printed or electronic form for physicians' review, signature, and corrections and for inclusion in patients' medical records. Translate medical jargon and abbreviations into their expanded forms to ensure the accuracy of patient and health-care facility records. Take dictation, using either shorthand or a stenotype machine or using headsets and transcribing machines. Convert dictated materials or rough notes to written form. Identify mistakes in reports and check with doctors to obtain the correct information. Perform data entry and data retrieval services, providing data for inclusion in medical records and for transmission to physicians. Produce medical reports, correspondence, records, patient-care information, statistics, medical research, and administrative material. Answer inquiries concerning the progress of medical cases within the limits of confidentiality laws. Set up and maintain medical files and databases, including records such as X-ray, lab, and procedure reports; medical histories; diagnostic workups; admission and discharge summaries; and clinical resumes. Perform a variety of clerical and office tasks, such as handling incoming and outgoing mail, completing and submitting insurance claims, typing, filing, and operating office machines. Decide which information should be included or excluded in reports. Receive patients, schedule appointments, and maintain patient records. Receive and screen telephone calls and visitors.

EYE OPENERS

Many medical transcriptionists telecommute from home-based offices.

- Annual earnings (average): $29,080
- Annual earnings (starting): $20,710
- Employed: 105,000
- Growth: 23.3%
- Annual job openings: 20,000

PREPARING FOR THE JOB

Education/training required: Postsecondary vocational training.

Programs: Medical transcription/transcriptionist training.

Knowledge/courses: Clerical practices; English language; medicine and dentistry; computers and electronics.

Licensure/certification: Certification available.

WORKING CONDITIONS

Physical: Indoors; sitting; using hands on objects, tools, or controls; repetitive motions.

Work settings: Hospitals, physicians' offices, transcription service offices, clinics, laboratories, medical libraries, government medical facilities, or home offices.

Other job characteristics: Need to be exact or accurate; repeat same tasks; automation; pace determined by speed of equipment.

TOP SKILLS

- Active listening
- Reading comprehension
- Time management
- Writing

OTHER FACTS

O*NET code: 31-9094.00

GOE information: Interest area: 08. Health Science. Work group: 08.02. Medicine and Surgery.

Personality type: No data available.

WHERE TO FIND OUT MORE

For information on a career as a medical transcriptionist, contact

➤ American Association for Medical Transcription, 4230 Kiernan Ave., Suite 130, Modesto, CA 95356. Internet: www.aamt.org

State employment service offices can provide information about job openings for medical transcriptionists.

video number

Surgical Technologists

QUICK LOOK

Assist in operations under the supervision of surgeons, registered nurses, or other surgical personnel. May help set up operating room, prepare and transport patients for surgery, adjust lights and equipment, and pass instruments and other supplies to surgeons and surgeon's assistants. Count sponges, needles, and instruments before and after operation. Scrub arms and hands and assist the surgical team in scrubbing and putting on gloves, masks, and surgical clothing. Position patients on the operating table and cover them with sterile surgical drapes to prevent exposure. Hold retractors, cut sutures, and perform other tasks as directed by surgeon during operation. Provide technical assistance to surgeons, surgical nurses, and anesthesiologists. Wash and sterilize equipment, using germicides and sterilizers. Prepare, care for, and dispose of tissue specimens taken for laboratory analysis. Clean and restock the operating room, placing equipment and supplies and arranging instruments according to instruction. Prepare dressings or bandages and apply or assist with their application following surgery. Operate, assemble, adjust, or monitor sterilizers, lights, suction machines, and diagnostic equipment to ensure proper operation. Monitor and continually assess operating room conditions, including patient and surgical team needs. Observe patients' vital signs to assess physical condition. Maintain supply of fluids, such as plasma, saline, blood, and glucose, for use during operations. Maintain files and records of surgical procedures.

EYE OPENERS

Training programs for surgical technologists last 9 to 24 months and lead to a certificate, diploma, or associate degree.

- Annual earnings (average): $34,830
- Annual earnings (starting): $24,530
- Employed: 84,000
- Growth: 29.5%
- Annual job openings: 12,000

PREPARING FOR THE JOB

Education/training required: Postsecondary vocational training.

Programs: Pathology/pathologist assistant training; surgical technology/technologist training.

Knowledge/courses: Medicine and dentistry; chemistry; philosophy and theology; psychology; customer and personal service; therapy and counseling; biology; education and training.

Licensure/certification: Certification available.

WORKING CONDITIONS

Physical: Indoors; contaminants; disease or infections; hazardous conditions; standing; using hands on objects, tools, or controls.

Work settings: Hospitals and other health-care facilities.

Other job characteristics: Need to be exact or accurate; errors have important consequences.

TOP SKILLS

- Troubleshooting
- Equipment selection
- Instructing
- Operation monitoring
- Science
- Reading comprehension

OTHER FACTS

O*NET code: 29-2055.00

GOE information: Interest area: 08. Health Science. Work group: 08.02. Medicine and Surgery.

Personality type: Realistic. Realistic occupations frequently involve work activities that include practical, hands-on problems and solutions. They often deal with plants, animals, and real-world materials like wood, tools, and machinery. Many of these occupations require working outside and do not involve a lot of paperwork or working closely with others.

WHERE TO FIND OUT MORE

For additional information on a career as a surgical technologist and a list of CAAHEP-accredited programs, contact

➤ Association of Surgical Technologists, 6 W. Dry Creek Circle, Suite 200, Littleton, CO 80120. Internet: www.ast.org

For information on becoming a Certified Surgical Technologist, contact

➤ National Board of Surgical Technology and Surgical Assisting, 6 W. Dry Creek Circle, Suite 100, Littleton, CO 80120. Internet: www.lcc-st.org

For information on becoming a Tech in Surgery-Certified (TS-C), contact:

➤ National Center for Competency Testing, 7007 College Blvd., Suite 705, Overland Park, KS 66211. Internet: www.ncctinc.com

Biological Technicians

QUICK LOOK

Assist biological and medical scientists in laboratories. **Set up, operate, and maintain laboratory instruments and equipment, monitor experiments, make observations, and calculate and record results. May analyze organic substances, such as blood, food, and drugs.** Keep detailed logs of all work-related activities. Monitor laboratory work to ensure compliance with set standards. Isolate, identify, and prepare specimens for examination. Use computers, computer-interfaced equipment, robotics, or high-tech industrial applications to perform work duties. Conduct research or assist in conducting research, including the collection of information and samples such as blood, water, soil, plants, and animals. Set up, adjust, calibrate, clean, maintain, and troubleshoot laboratory and field equipment. Provide technical support and services for scientists and engineers working in fields such as agriculture, environmental science, resource management, biology, and health sciences. Clean, maintain, and prepare supplies and work areas. Participate in the research, development, or manufacturing of medicinal and pharmaceutical preparations. Conduct standardized biological, microbiological, or biochemical tests and laboratory analyses to evaluate the quantity or quality of physical or chemical substances in food or other products. Analyze experimental data and interpret results to write reports and summaries of findings. Measure or weigh compounds and solutions for use in testing or animal feed. Monitor and observe experiments, recording production and test data for evaluation by research personnel. Examine animals and specimens to detect the presence of disease or other problems. Conduct or supervise operational programs such as fish hatcheries, greenhouses, and livestock production programs. Feed livestock or laboratory animals.

EYE OPENERS

Biological technicians usually begin work as trainees in routine positions under the direct supervision of a scientist or a more experienced technician.

- Annual earnings (average): $34,270
- Annual earnings (starting): $22,480
- Employed: 64,000
- Growth: 17.2%
- Annual job openings: 8,000

PREPARING FOR THE JOB

Education/training required: Associate degree.

Programs: Biology technician training/biotechnology laboratory technician training.

Knowledge/courses: Chemistry; biology; mathematics.

Licensure/certification: Certification available.

WORKING CONDITIONS

Physical: Indoors; standing; using hands on objects, tools, or controls; repetitive motions.

Work settings: Usually laboratories; sometimes in the field.

Other job characteristics: Need to be exact or accurate; repeat same tasks; errors have important consequences.

OTHER FACTS

O*NET code: 19-4021.00

GOE information: Interest area: 08. Health Science. Work group: 08.06. Medical Technology.

Personality type: Realistic. Realistic occupations frequently involve work activities that include practical, hands-on problems and solutions. They often deal with plants, animals, and real-world materials like wood, tools, and machinery. Many of the occupations require working outside and do not involve a lot of paperwork or working closely with others.

TOP SKILLS

- Science
- Equipment maintenance
- Active learning
- Quality control analysis
- Troubleshooting
- Mathematics

WHERE TO FIND OUT MORE

For career information, contact

➤ Federation of American Societies for Experimental Biology, 9650 Rockville Pike, Bethesda, MD 20814. Internet: www.faseb.org/

Cardiovascular Technologists and Technicians

QUICK LOOK

Conduct tests on pulmonary or cardiovascular systems of patients for diagnostic purposes. May conduct or assist in electrocardiograms, cardiac catheterizations, pulmonary function, lung capacity, and similar tests. Monitor patients' blood pressure and heart rate, using electrocardiogram (EKG) equipment, during diagnostic and therapeutic procedures to notify the physician if something appears wrong. Monitor patients' comfort and safety during tests, alerting physicians to abnormalities or changes in patient responses. Explain testing procedures to patients to obtain cooperation and reduce anxiety. Prepare reports of diagnostic procedures for interpretation by a physician. Observe gauges, recorder, and video screens of data analysis system during imaging of the cardiovascular system. Conduct electrocardiogram (EKG), phonocardiogram, echocardiogram, stress testing, or other cardiovascular tests to record patients' cardiac activity, using specialized electronic test equipment, recording devices, and laboratory instruments. Obtain and record patient identification, medical history, or test results. Prepare and position patients for testing. Attach electrodes to patients' chests, arms, and legs; connect electrodes to leads from an electrocardiogram (EKG) machine; and operate an EKG machine to obtain a reading. Adjust equipment and controls according to physicians' orders or established protocol. Check, test, and maintain cardiology equipment, making minor repairs when necessary, to ensure proper operation. Supervise and train other cardiology technologists and students. Assist physicians in diagnosis of cardiac problems and implementation of peripheral vascular treatments, such as balloon angioplasties to treat blood vessel blockages. Operate diagnostic imaging equipment to produce contrast-enhanced radiographs of the heart and cardiovascular system. Inject contrast medium into patients' blood vessels. Observe ultrasound display screen and listen to signals to record vascular information such as blood pressure, limb volume changes, oxygen saturation, and cerebral circulation. Assess cardiac physiology and calculate valve areas from blood flow velocity measurements. Compare measurements of heart wall thickness and chamber sizes to standard norms to identify abnormalities. Activate a fluoroscope and camera to produce images used to guide a catheter through the cardiovascular system.

EYE OPENERS

Employment of most specialties will grow, but fewer EKG technicians will be needed.

- Annual earnings (average): $40,420
- Annual earnings (starting): $22,810
- Employed: 45,000
- Growth: 32.6%
- Annual job openings: 5,000

PREPARING FOR THE JOB

Education/training required: Associate degree.

Programs: Cardiopulmonary technology/technologist training; cardiovascular technology/technologist training; electrocardiograph technology/technician training; perfusion technology/perfusionist training.

Knowledge/courses: Medicine and dentistry; customer and personal service; psychology; physics; biology; therapy and counseling; education and training; mathematics.

Licensure/certification: Certification available for certain specializations.

WORKING CONDITIONS

Physical: Indoors; radiation; disease or infections; standing; walking and running; using hands on objects, tools, or controls.

Work settings: Hospitals and health-care facilities, perhaps in catheterization laboratories.

Other job characteristics: Need to be exact or accurate; repeat same tasks; errors have important consequences.

TOP SKILLS

- Operation monitoring
- Science
- Equipment maintenance
- Instructing
- Service orientation
- Operation and control

OTHER FACTS

O*NET code: 29-2031.00

GOE information: Interest area: 08. Health Science. Work group: 08.06. Medical Technology.

Personality type: Investigative. Investigative occupations frequently involve working with ideas and require an extensive amount of thinking. These occupations can involve searching for facts and figuring out problems.

WHERE TO FIND OUT MORE

For information about a career and programs in cardiovascular technology, contact

➤ Alliance of Cardiovascular Professionals, P.O. Box 2007, Midlothian, VA 23112. Internet: www.acp-online.org

➤ Committee on Accreditation for Allied Health Education Programs, 1361 Park St., Clearwater, FL 33756. Internet: www.caahep.org

➤ Joint Review Committee on Education in Cardiovascular Technology, 1248 Harwood Rd., Bedford, TX 76021. Internet: www.jrccvt.org

Dental Hygienists

QUICK LOOK

Clean teeth and examine oral areas, head, and neck for signs of oral disease. May educate patients on oral hygiene, take and develop X-rays, or apply fluoride or sealants. Clean calcareous deposits, accretions, and stains from teeth and beneath margins of gums, using dental instruments. Feel and visually examine gums for sores and signs of disease. Chart conditions of decay and disease for diagnosis and treatment by a dentist. Feel lymph nodes under patient's chin to detect swelling or tenderness that could indicate presence of oral cancer. Apply fluorides and other cavity-preventing agents to arrest dental decay. Examine gums, using probes, to locate periodontal recessed gums and signs of gum disease. Expose and develop X-ray film. Provide clinical services and health education to improve and maintain oral health of schoolchildren. Remove excess cement from coronal surfaces of teeth. Make impressions for study casts. Place, carve, and finish amalgam restorations. Administer local anesthetic agents. Conduct dental health clinics for community groups to augment services of a dentist. Remove sutures and dressings. Place and remove rubber dams, matrices, and temporary restorations.

── EYE OPENERS ──

More than half of dental hygienists work part-time, and flexible scheduling is a distinctive feature of this job.

- Annual earnings (average): $60,890
- Annual earnings (starting): $38,470
- Employed: 158,000
- Growth: 43.3%
- Annual job openings: 17,000

PREPARING FOR THE JOB

Education/training required: Associate degree.

Programs: Dental hygiene/hygienist training.

Knowledge/courses: Biology; medicine and dentistry; chemistry; psychology; sales and marketing; therapy and counseling; customer and personal service; production and processing.

Licensure/certification: Licensure required.

WORKING CONDITIONS

Physical: Indoors; radiation; disease or infections; sitting; using hands on objects, tools, or controls; repetitive motions.

Work settings: Dentists' offices.

Other job characteristics: Need to be exact or accurate; repeat same tasks; errors have important consequences.

OTHER FACTS

O*NET code: 29-2021.00

GOE information: Interest area: 08. Health Science. Work group: 08.03. Dentistry.

---— TOP SKILLS ——---

- Active learning
- Time management
- Persuasion
- Reading comprehension
- Science
- Social perceptiveness

Personality type: Social. Social occupations frequently involve working with, communicating with, and teaching people. These occupations often involve helping or providing service to others.

WHERE TO FIND OUT MORE

For information on a career in dental hygiene, including educational requirements, contact

➤ Division of Education, American Dental Hygienists' Association, 444 N. Michigan Ave., Suite 3400, Chicago, IL 60611. Internet: www.adha.org

For information about accredited programs and educational requirements, contact

➤ American Dental Association, Commission on Dental Accreditation, 211 E. Chicago Ave., Chicago, IL 60611-2678. Internet: www.ada.org

The state board of dental examiners in each state can supply information on licensing requirements.

Associate Degree

QUICK LOOK

Produce ultrasonic recordings of internal organs for use by physicians. Decide which images to include, looking for differences between healthy and pathological areas. Observe screen during scan to ensure that image produced is satisfactory for diagnostic purposes, making adjustments to equipment as required. Observe and care for patients throughout examinations to ensure their safety and comfort. Provide sonogram and oral or written summary of technical findings to physician for use in medical diagnosis. Operate ultrasound equipment to produce and record images of the motion, shape, and composition of blood, organs, tissues, and bodily masses, such as fluid accumulations. Select appropriate equipment settings and adjust patients' positions to obtain the best sites and angles. Determine whether scope of exam should be extended based on findings. Process and code film from procedures and complete appropriate documentation. Obtain and record accurate patient history, including prior test results and information from physical examinations. Prepare patients for exams by explaining the procedure, transferring them to the ultrasound table, scrubbing their skin and applying gel, and positioning them properly. Record and store suitable images, using the camera unit connected to the ultrasound equipment. Coordinate work with physicians and other health-care team members and provide assistance during invasive procedures. Maintain records that include patient information; sonographs and interpretations; files of correspondence, publications, and regulations; or quality assurance records such as pathology, biopsy, or post-operative reports. Perform legal and ethical duties, including preparing safety and accident reports, obtaining written consent from patients to perform invasive procedures, and reporting symptoms of abuse and neglect. Supervise and train students and other medical sonographers. Maintain stock and supplies, preparing supplies for special examinations and ordering supplies when necessary. Clean, check, and maintain sonographic equipment, submitting maintenance requests or performing minor repairs as necessary. Perform clerical duties such as scheduling exams and special procedures, keeping records, and archiving computerized images.

— EYE OPENERS —

Sonographers may train in hospitals, vocational-technical institutions, colleges and universities, and the military.

- Annual earnings (average): $54,370
- Annual earnings (starting): $38,970
- Employed: 42,000
- Growth: 34.8%
- Annual job openings: 5,000

PREPARING FOR THE JOB

Education/training required: Associate degree.

Programs: Allied health diagnostic, intervention, and treatment professions; diagnostic medical sonography/sonographer and ultrasound technician training.

Knowledge/courses: Medicine and dentistry; biology; physics; therapy and counseling; education and training; clerical practices; customer and personal service; English language.

Licensure/certification: Certification available.

WORKING CONDITIONS

Physical: Indoors; cramped work space, awkward positions; disease or infections; using hands on objects, tools, or controls; bending or twisting the body; repetitive motions.

Work settings: Offices in hospitals and other health-care facilities.

Other job characteristics: Need to be exact or accurate; repeat same tasks; errors have important consequences.

TOP SKILLS

- Operation and control
- Social perceptiveness
- Reading comprehension
- Science
- Learning strategies
- Instructing

OTHER FACTS

O*NET code: 29-2032.00

GOE information: Interest area: 08. Health Science. Work group: 08.06. Medical Technology.

Personality type: No data available.

WHERE TO FIND OUT MORE

For information on a career as a diagnostic medical sonographer, contact

➤ Society of Diagnostic Medical Sonography, 2745 Dallas Pkwy., Suite 350, Plano, TX 75093-8730. Internet: www.sdms.org

For information on becoming a registered diagnostic medical sonographer, contact

➤ American Registry for Diagnostic Medical Sonography, 51 Monroe St., Plaza East One, Rockville, MD 20850-2400. Internet: www.ardms.org

QUICK LOOK

Collect, identify, classify, and analyze physical evidence related to criminal investigations. **Perform tests on weapons or substances, such as fiber, hair, and tissue to determine their significance to an investigation. May testify as expert witnesses on evidence or crime laboratory techniques. May serve as specialists in area of expertise, such as ballistics, fingerprinting, handwriting, or biochemistry.** Testify in court about investigative and analytical methods and findings. Keep records and prepare reports detailing findings, investigative methods, and laboratory techniques. Interpret laboratory findings and test results to identify and classify substances, materials, and other evidence collected at crime scenes. Operate and maintain laboratory equipment and apparatus. Prepare solutions, reagents, and sample formulations needed for laboratory work. Analyze and classify biological fluids, using DNA typing or serological techniques. Collect evidence from crime scenes, storing it in conditions that preserve its integrity. Identify and quantify drugs and poisons found in biological fluids and tissues, in foods, and at crime scenes. Analyze handwritten and machine-produced textual evidence to decipher altered or obliterated text or to determine authorship, age, or source. Reconstruct crime scenes to determine relationships among pieces of evidence. Examine DNA samples to determine whether they match other samples. Collect impressions of dust from surfaces to obtain and identify fingerprints. Analyze gunshot residue and bullet paths to determine how shootings occurred. Visit morgues, examine scenes of crimes, or contact other sources to obtain evidence or information to be used in investigations. Examine physical evidence such as hair, fiber, wood, or soil residues to obtain information about its source and composition. Determine types of bullets used in a shooting and whether they were fired from a specific weapon. Examine firearms to determine mechanical condition and legal status and perform restoration work on damaged firearms to obtain information such as serial numbers. Confer with ballistics, fingerprinting, handwriting, document, electronics, medical, chemical, or metallurgical experts concerning evidence and its interpretation. Interpret the pharmacological effects of a drug or a combination of drugs on an individual. Compare objects such as tools with impression marks to determine whether a specific object is responsible for a specific mark.

— EYE OPENERS —

Job-seekers with a four-year degree in forensic science will enjoy much better opportunities than those with only a two-year degree.

- Annual earnings (average): $44,590
- Annual earnings (starting): $27,350
- Employed: 10,000
- Growth: 36.4%
- Annual job openings: 2,000

Preparing for the Job

Education/training required: Associate degree.

Programs: Forensic Science and Technology.

Knowledge/courses: Chemistry; law and government; biology; public safety and security; English language; clerical practices; customer and personal service; psychology.

Licensure/certification: Certification available in some specializations.

Working Conditions

Physical: Indoors; contaminants; disease or infections; hazardous conditions; sitting.

Work settings: Indoors, usually in laboratories, and either indoors or outdoors at crime scenes.

Other job characteristics: Need to be exact or accurate; errors have important consequences.

Other Facts

O*NET code: 19-4092.00

GOE information: Interest area: 12. Law and Public Safety. Work group: 12.04. Law Enforcement and Public Safety.

Personality type: Investigative. Investigative occupations frequently involve working with ideas and require an extensive amount of thinking. These occupations can involve searching for facts and figuring out problems.

TOP SKILLS

- Science
- Quality control analysis
- Troubleshooting
- Speaking
- Active learning
- Reading comprehension

Where to Find Out More

For career information and a list of undergraduate, graduate, and doctoral programs in forensic sciences, contact

➤ American Academy of Forensic Sciences, 410 N. 21st St., Colorado Springs, CO, 80904. Internet: www.aafs.org

Medical and Clinical Laboratory Technicians

QUICK LOOK

Perform routine medical laboratory tests for the diagnosis, treatment, and prevention of disease. May work under the supervision of a medical technologist. Conduct chemical analyses of body fluids, such as blood and urine, using a microscope or an automatic analyzer to detect abnormalities or diseases. Enter findings into a computer. Set up, adjust, maintain, and clean medical laboratory equipment. Analyze the results of tests and experiments to ensure conformity to specifications, using special mechanical and electrical devices. Analyze and record test data to issue reports that use charts, graphs, and narratives. Conduct blood tests for transfusion purposes and perform blood counts. Perform medical research to further control and cure disease. Obtain specimens, cultivating, isolating, and identifying microorganisms for analysis. Examine cells stained with dye to locate abnormalities. Collect blood or tissue samples from patients, observing principles of asepsis to obtain blood sample. Consult with a pathologist to determine a final diagnosis when abnormal cells are found. Inoculate fertilized eggs, broths, or other bacteriological media with organisms. Cut, stain, and mount tissue samples for examination by pathologists. Supervise and instruct other technicians and laboratory assistants. Prepare standard volumetric solutions and reagents to be combined with samples, following standardized formulas or experimental procedures. Prepare vaccines and serums by standard laboratory methods, testing for virus inactivity and sterility. Test raw materials, processes, and finished products to determine quality and quantity of materials or characteristics of a substance.

— EYE OPENERS —

Job opportunities for this occupation are expected to be excellent.

- Annual earnings (average): $31,700
- Annual earnings (starting): $20,700
- Employed: 147,000
- Growth: 25.0%
- Annual job openings: 14,000

PREPARING FOR THE JOB

Education/training required: Associate degree.

Programs: Blood bank technology specialist training; clinical/medical laboratory assistant training; clinical/medical laboratory technician training; hematology technology/technician training; histologic technician training.

Knowledge/courses: Medicine and dentistry; therapy and counseling; biology; clerical practices.

Licensure/certification: Certification available; licensure required in some states.

WORKING CONDITIONS

Physical: Indoors; disease or infections; standing; walking and running; using hands on objects, tools, or controls.

Work settings: Laboratories in large hospitals or independent laboratories.

Other job characteristics: Need to be exact or accurate; errors have important consequences; repeat same tasks.

TOP SKILLS

- Science
- Equipment maintenance
- Troubleshooting
- Operation monitoring
- Quality control analysis
- Operation and control

OTHER FACTS

O*NET code: 29-2012.00

GOE information: Interest area: 08. Health Science. Work group: 08.06. Medical Technology.

Personality type: Realistic. Realistic occupations frequently involve work activities that include practical, hands-on problems and solutions. They often deal with plants, animals, and real-world materials like wood, tools, and machinery. Many of these occupations require working outside and do not involve a lot of paperwork or working closely with others.

WHERE TO FIND OUT MORE

For information on accredited programs and certification, contact

➤ National Accrediting Agency for Clinical Laboratory Sciences, 8410 W. Bryn Mawr Ave., Suite 670, Chicago, IL 60631. Internet: www.naacls.org

➤ American Association of Bioanalysts, Board of Registry, 906 Olive St., Suite 1200, St. Louis, MO 63101-1434. Internet: www.aab.org

➤ American Medical Technologists, 10700 W. Higgins Rd., Suite 150, Rosemont, IL 60018. Internet: www.amt1.com

➤ American Society for Clinical Pathology, 33 W. Monroe St., Suite 1600, Chicago, IL 60603-5617. Internet: www.ascp.org

➤ National Credentialing Agency for Laboratory Personnel, P.O. Box 15945-289, Lenexa, KS 66285. Internet: www.nca-info.org

Medical Records and Health Information Technicians

QUICK LOOK

Compile, process, and maintain medical records of hospital and clinic patients in a manner consistent with medical, administrative, ethical, legal, and regulatory requirements of the health care system. Process, maintain, compile, and report patient information for health requirements and standards. Protect the security of medical records to ensure that confidentiality is maintained. Process patient admission and discharge documents. Review records for completeness, accuracy, and compliance with regulations. Compile and maintain patients' medical records to document condition and treatment and to provide data for research or cost control and care improvement efforts. Enter data such as demographic characteristics, history and extent of disease, diagnostic procedures, and treatment into a computer. Release information to persons and agencies according to regulations. Plan, develop, maintain, and operate a variety of health record indexes and storage and retrieval systems to collect, classify, store, and analyze information. Manage the medical records department and supervise clerical workers, directing and controlling activities of personnel in this department. Transcribe medical reports. Identify, compile, abstract, and code patient data, using standard classification systems. Resolve or clarify codes and diagnoses with conflicting, missing, or unclear information by consulting with doctors or others or by participating in the coding team's regular meetings. Train medical records staff. Assign the patient to diagnosis-related groups (DRGs), using appropriate computer software. Post medical insurance billings. Process and prepare business and government forms. Contact discharged patients, their families, and physicians to maintain registry with follow-up information, such as quality of life and length of survival of cancer patients. Prepare statistical reports, narrative reports, and graphic presentations of information, such as tumor registry data, for use by hospital staff, researchers, or other users. Consult classification manuals to locate information about disease processes. Compile medical care and census data for statistical reports on diseases treated, surgery performed, or use of hospital beds. Develop in-service educational materials.

─ EYE OPENERS ─

This is one of the few health occupations in which there is little or no direct contact with patients.

- Annual earnings (average): $26,690
- Annual earnings (starting): $18,410
- Employed: 159,000
- Growth: 28.9%
- Annual job openings: 14,000

PREPARING FOR THE JOB

Education/training required: Associate degree.

Programs: Health information/medical records technology/technician training; medical insurance coding specialist/coder training.

Knowledge/courses: Clerical practices; personnel and human resources; administration and management; computers and electronics.

Licensure/certification: Certification available.

WORKING CONDITIONS

Physical: Indoors; noisy; sitting; using hands on objects, tools, or controls; repetitive motions.

Work settings: Hospitals and other health-care facilities and physicians' offices.

Other job characteristics: Need to be exact or accurate; repeat same tasks; automation.

```
┌──────── TOP SKILLS ────────┐
│                             │
│  • Systems evaluation       │
│  • Active listening         │
│  • Reading comprehension    │
│  • Instructing              │
│  • Critical thinking        │
│  • Time management          │
│                             │
└─────────────────────────────┘
```

OTHER FACTS

O*NET code: 29-2071.00

GOE information: Interest area: 08. Health Science. Work group: 08.06. Medical Technology.

Personality type: Conventional. Conventional occupations frequently involve following set procedures and routines. These occupations can include working with data and details more than with ideas. Usually there is a clear line of authority to follow.

WHERE TO FIND OUT MORE

Information on careers in medical records and health information technology is available from

➤ American Health Information Management Association, 233 N. Michigan Ave., Suite 2150, Chicago, IL 60601-5800. Internet: www.ahima.org

➤ American Academy of Professional Coders, 2480 S. 3850 W., Suite B, Salt Lake City, UT 84120. Internet: www.aapc.com

➤ National Cancer Registrars Association, 1340 Braddock Pl., #203, Alexandria, VA 22314. Internet: www.ncra-usa.org

Associate Degree

Nuclear Medicine Technologists

QUICK LOOK

Prepare, administer, and measure radioactive isotopes in therapeutic, diagnostic, and tracer studies utilizing a variety of radioisotope equipment. Prepare stock solutions of radioactive materials and calculate doses to be administered by radiologists. Subject patients to radiation. Execute blood volume, red cell survival, and fat absorption studies following standard laboratory techniques. Calculate, measure, and record radiation dosage or radiopharmaceuticals received, used, and disposed, using a computer and following a physician's prescription. Detect and map radiopharmaceuticals in patients' bodies, using a camera to produce photographic or computer images. Explain test procedures and safety precautions to patients and provide them with assistance during test procedures. Administer radiopharmaceuticals or radiation to patients to detect or treat diseases, using radioisotope equipment, under direction of a physician. Produce a computer-generated or film image for interpretation by a physician. Process cardiac function studies, using a computer. Dispose of radioactive materials and store radiopharmaceuticals, following radiation safety procedures. Record and process results of procedures. Prepare stock radiopharmaceuticals, adhering to safety standards that minimize radiation exposure to workers and patients. Maintain and calibrate radioisotope and laboratory equipment. Gather information on patients' illnesses and medical history to guide the choice of diagnostic procedures for therapy. Measure glandular activity, blood volume, red cell survival, and radioactivity of patient, using scanners, Geiger counters, scintillometers, and other laboratory equipment. Train and supervise student or subordinate nuclear medicine technologists. Position radiation fields, radiation beams, and patient to allow for most effective treatment of patient's disease, using computer. Add radioactive substances to biological specimens, such as blood, urine, and feces, to determine therapeutic drug or hormone levels. Develop treatment procedures for nuclear medicine treatment programs.

— EYE OPENERS —

Nuclear medicine technology programs range in length from one to four years and lead to a certificate, an associate degree, or a bachelor's degree.

- Annual earnings (average): $59,670
- Annual earnings (starting): $44,650
- Employed: 18,000
- Growth: 21.5%
- Annual job openings: 2,000

PREPARING FOR THE JOB

Education/training required: Associate degree.

Programs: Nuclear Medical Technology/Technologist Training; Radiation Protection/Health Physics Technician Training.

Knowledge/courses: Medicine and dentistry; biology; physics; chemistry; customer and personal service; computers and electronics; psychology; mathematics.

Licensure/certification: Certification or licensure required in some states.

WORKING CONDITIONS

Physical: Indoors; contaminants; radiation; disease or infections; standing; using hands on objects, tools, or controls.

Work settings: Hospitals and other health-care facilities.

Other job characteristics: Need to be exact or accurate; errors have important consequences; repeat same tasks.

OTHER FACTS

O*NET code: 29-2033.00

GOE information: Interest area: 08. Health Science. Work group: 08.06. Medical Technology.

— **TOP SKILLS** —

- Science
- Operation monitoring
- Operation and control
- Quality control analysis
- Social perceptiveness
- Service orientation

Personality type: Investigative. Investigative occupations frequently involve working with ideas and require an extensive amount of thinking. These occupations can involve searching for facts and figuring out problems.

WHERE TO FIND OUT MORE

Additional information on a career as a nuclear medicine technologist is available from

➤ Society of Nuclear Medicine, 1850 Samuel Morse Dr., Reston, VA 20190-5316. Internet: www.snm.org

➤ American Society of Radiologic Technologists, 15000 Central Ave. SE, Albuquerque, NM 87123-3917. Internet: www.asrt.org

For a list of accredited programs in nuclear medicine technology, contact

➤ Joint Review Committee on Educational Programs in Nuclear Medicine Technology, 2000 W. Danforth Rd., Suite 130, #203, Edmond, OK 73003. Internet: www.jrcnmt.org

Occupational Therapist Assistants

QUICK LOOK

Assist occupational therapists in providing occupational therapy treatments and procedures. May, in accordance with state laws, assist in development of treatment plans, carry
out routine functions, direct activity programs, and document the progress of treatments.
Observe and record patients' progress, attitudes, and behavior and maintain this information
in patient records. Maintain and promote a positive attitude toward patients and their treatment programs. Monitor patients' performance in therapy activities, providing encourage-
ment. Select therapy activities to fit patients' needs and capabilities. Aid patients in dressing
and grooming themselves. Instruct, or assist in instructing, patients and families in home programs, basic living skills, and the care and use of adaptive equipment. Evaluate the daily living skills and capacities of physically,
developmentally, or emotionally disabled
patients. Implement, or assist occupational
therapists with implementing, treatment plans
designed to help patients function independently. Report to supervisors, verbally or in writing, on patients' progress, attitudes, and
behavior. Alter treatment programs to obtain
better results if treatment is not having the
intended effect. Work under the direction of
occupational therapists to plan, implement,
and administer educational, vocational, and
recreational programs that restore and enhance
performance in individuals with functional
impairments. Design, fabricate, and repair
assistive devices and make adaptive changes to
equipment and environments. Assemble, clean, and maintain equipment and materials for
patient use. Teach patients how to deal constructively with their emotions. Perform clerical
duties such as scheduling appointments, collecting data, and documenting health insurance
billings. Transport patients to and from the occupational therapy work area. Demonstrate
therapy techniques such as manual and creative arts or games. Order any needed educational
or treatment supplies. Assist educational specialists or clinical psychologists in administering
situational or diagnostic tests to measure a patient's abilities or progress.

EYE OPENERS

Applicants to occupational therapist assistant programs can improve their chances of
admission by taking high school courses in
biology and health and by performing vol-
unteer work in nursing care facilities, occupational or physical therapists' offices, or
other health care settings.

- Annual earnings (average): $39,750
- Annual earnings (starting): $24,670
- Employed: 21,000
- Growth: 34.1%
- Annual job openings: 2,000

PREPARING FOR THE JOB

Education/training required: Associate degree.

Programs: Occupational therapist assistant training.

Knowledge/courses: Therapy and counseling; psychology; sociology and anthropology; philosophy and theology; medicine and dentistry; biology; customer and personal service; public safety and security.

Licensure/certification: Certification available and required in some states.

WORKING CONDITIONS

Physical: Indoors; disease or infections; standing; walking and running; using hands on objects, tools, or controls; bending or twisting the body.

Work settings: Hospitals, therapists' offices, and other health-care facilities.

Other job characteristics: Need to be exact or accurate; repeat same tasks.

OTHER FACTS

O*NET code: 31-2011.00

GOE information: Interest area: 08. Health Science. Work group: 08.07. Medical Therapy.

```
┌──────── TOP SKILLS ────────┐
│                            │
│  • Social perceptiveness   │
│  • Operations analysis     │
│  • Persuasion              │
│  • Service orientation     │
│  • Writing                 │
│  • Time management         │
│                            │
└────────────────────────────┘
```

Personality type: Social. Social occupations frequently involve working with, communicating with, and teaching people. These occupations often involve helping or providing service to others.

WHERE TO FIND OUT MORE

For information on a career as an occupational therapist assistant or aide and a list of accredited programs, contact

➤ American Occupational Therapy Association, 4720 Montgomery Lane, P.O. Box 31220, Bethesda, MD 20824-1220. Internet: www.aota.org

Associate Degree

Physical Therapist Assistants

QUICK LOOK

Assist physical therapists in providing physical therapy treatments and procedures. May, in accordance with state laws, assist in the development of treatment plans, carry out routine functions, document the progress of treatment, and modify specific treatments in accordance with patient status and within the scope of treatment plans established by a physical therapist. Instruct, motivate, safeguard, and assist patients as they practice exercises and functional activities. Confer with physical therapy staff or others to discuss and evaluate patient information for planning, modifying, and coordinating treatment. Administer active and passive manual therapeutic exercises; therapeutic massage; and heat, light, sound, water, and electrical modality treatments such as ultrasound. Observe patients during treatments to compile and evaluate data on patients' responses and progress and report to a physical therapist. Measure patients' range of joint motion, body parts, and vital signs to determine effects of treatments or for patient evaluations. Secure patients into or onto therapy equipment. Fit patients for orthopedic braces, prostheses, and supportive devices such as crutches. Train patients in the use of orthopedic braces, prostheses, or supportive devices. Transport patients to and from treatment areas, lifting and transferring them according to positioning requirements. Monitor operation of equipment and record use of equipment and administration of treatment. Clean work area and check and store equipment after treatment. Assist patients in dressing, undressing, or putting on and removing supportive devices such as braces, splints, and slings. Administer traction to relieve neck and back pain, using intermittent and static traction equipment. Perform clerical duties, such as taking inventory, ordering supplies, answering telephone, taking messages, and filling out forms. Prepare treatment areas and electrotherapy equipment for use by physiotherapists. Perform postural drainage, percussions, and vibrations and teach deep breathing exercises to treat respiratory conditions.

EYE OPENERS

Not all states require licensure or registration in order for a physical therapist assistant to practice. The states that require licensure set specific criteria for education and examinations.

- Annual earnings (average): $39,490
- Annual earnings (starting): $25,640
- Employed: 59,000
- Growth: 44.2%
- Annual job openings: 7,000

Preparing for the Job

Education/training required: Associate degree.

Programs: Physical therapist assistant training.

Knowledge/courses: Therapy and counseling; psychology; medicine and dentistry; education and training; sociology and anthropology; biology; philosophy and theology; customer and personal service.

Licensure/certification: Certification available and required in many states.

Working Conditions

Physical: Indoors; disease or infections; standing; walking and running; using hands on objects, tools, or controls; bending or twisting the body.

Work settings: Hospitals, therapists' offices, and other health-care facilities.

Other job characteristics: Need to be exact or accurate; errors have important consequences.

Other Facts

O*NET code: 31-2021.00

GOE information: Interest area: 08. Health Science. Work group: 08.07. Medical Therapy.

Personality type: Social. Social occupations frequently involve working with, communicating with, and teaching people. These occupations often involve helping or providing service to others.

Where to Find Out More

To obtain career information about physical therapist assistants and a list of schools offering accredited programs, contact

➤ American Physical Therapy Association, 1111 N. Fairfax St., Alexandria, VA 22314-1488. Internet: www.apta.org

Associate Degree

Radiation Therapists

QUICK LOOK

Provide radiation therapy to patients as prescribed by a radiologist according to established practices and standards. Duties may include reviewing the prescription and diagnosis; acting as liaison with physician and supportive care personnel; preparing equipment; and maintaining records, reports, and files. May assist in dosimetry procedures and tumor localization. Administer prescribed doses of radiation to specific body parts, using radiation therapy equipment according to established practices and standards. Position patients for treatment with accuracy according to prescription. Enter data into computer and set controls to operate and adjust equipment and regulate dosage. Follow principles of radiation protection for patient, self, and others. Maintain records, reports, and files as required, including such information as radiation dosages, equipment settings, and patients' reactions. Review prescription, diagnosis, patient chart, and identification. Conduct most treatment sessions independently in accordance with the long-term treatment plan and under the general direction of the patient's physician. Check radiation therapy equipment to ensure proper operation. Observe and reassure patients during treatment and report unusual reactions to physician or turn off equipment if unexpected adverse reactions occur. Check for side effects such as skin irritation, nausea, and hair loss to assess patients' reaction to treatment. Educate, prepare, and reassure patients and their families by answering questions, providing physical assistance, and reinforcing physicians' advice regarding treatment reactions and post-treatment care. Calculate actual treatment dosages delivered during each session. Prepare and construct equipment, such as immobilization, treatment, and protection devices. Photograph treated area of patient and process film. Help physicians, radiation oncologists, and clinical physicists to prepare physical and technical aspects of radiation treatment plans, using information about patient condition and anatomy. Train and supervise student or subordinate radiotherapy technologists. Provide assistance to other health-care personnel during dosimetry procedures and tumor localization. Implement appropriate follow-up care plans. Act as liaison with physicist and supportive care personnel. Store, sterilize, or prepare the special applicators containing the radioactive substance implanted by the physician. Assist in the preparation of sealed radioactive materials, such as cobalt, radium, cesium, and isotopes, for use in radiation treatments.

━ EYE OPENERS ━

Job applicants who are certified and who possess a bachelor's or an associate degree or a certificate in radiation therapy should have the best prospects.

- Annual earnings (average): $62,340
- Annual earnings (starting): $42,380
- Employed: 15,000
- Growth: 26.3%
- Annual job openings: 1,000

PREPARING FOR THE JOB

Education/training required: Associate degree.

Programs: Medical radiologic technology/science—radiation therapist training.

Knowledge/courses: Medicine and dentistry; biology; physics; psychology; therapy and counseling; customer and personal service; mathematics; education and training.

Licensure/certification: Certification available; licensure required in some states.

WORKING CONDITIONS

Physical: Indoors; disease or infections; standing; walking and running; using hands on objects, tools, or controls; repetitive motions.

Work settings: Hospitals or cancer treatment centers.

Other job characteristics: Need to be exact or accurate; repeat same tasks; errors have important consequences; pace determined by speed of equipment.

OTHER FACTS

O*NET code: 29-1124.00

GOE information: Interest area: 08. Health Science. Work group: 08.07. Medical Therapy.

---- TOP SKILLS ----

- Operation monitoring
- Operation and control
- Technology design
- Time management
- Science
- Management of personnel resources

Personality type: Social. Social occupations frequently involve working with, communicating with, and teaching people. These occupations often involve helping or providing service to others.

WHERE TO FIND OUT MORE

For information on certification and on accredited radiation therapy programs, contact

➤ The American Registry of Radiologic Technologists, 1255 Northland Dr., St. Paul, MN 55120-1155. Internet: www.arrt.org

For information on careers in radiation therapy, contact

➤ American Society of Radiologic Technologists, 15000 Central Ave. SE, Albuquerque, NM 87123-3917. Internet: www.asrt.org

Associate Degree

Radiologic Technicians

QUICK LOOK

Maintain and use equipment and supplies necessary to show portions of the human body on X-ray film or a fluoroscopic screen for diagnostic purposes. Use beam-restrictive devices and patient-shielding techniques to minimize radiation exposure to patient and staff. Position X-ray equipment and adjust controls to set exposure factors, such as time and distance. Position patient on examining table and set up and adjust equipment to obtain optimum view of specific body area as requested by a physician. Determine patients' X-ray needs by reading requests or instructions from physicians. Make exposures necessary for the requested procedures, rejecting and repeating work that does not meet established standards. Process exposed radiographs, using film processors or computer-generated methods. Explain procedures to patients to reduce anxieties and obtain cooperation. Perform procedures such as linear tomography; mammography; sonograms; joint and cyst aspirations; routine contrast studies; routine fluoroscopy; and examinations of the head, trunk, and extremities under supervision of a physician. Prepare and set up the X-ray room for patients. Assure that sterile supplies, contrast materials, catheters, and other required equipment are present and in working order, requisitioning materials as necessary. Maintain records of patients examined, examinations performed, views taken, and technical factors used. Provide assistance to physicians or other technologists in the performance of more complex procedures. Monitor equipment operation and report malfunctioning equipment to supervisor. Provide students and other technologists with suggestions of additional views, alternate positioning, or improved techniques to ensure the images produced are of the highest quality. Coordinate work of other technicians or technologists when procedures require more than one person. Assist with on-the-job training of new employees and students and provide input to supervisors regarding training performance. Maintain a current file of examination protocols. Operate mobile X-ray equipment in operating room, in emergency room, or at a patient's bedside. Provide assistance in radiopharmaceutical administration, monitoring patients' vital signs and notifying the radiologist of any relevant changes.

— EYE OPENERS —

Job opportunities for radiologic technicians are expected to be favorable. Some employers report difficulty hiring sufficient numbers of trained workers.

- Annual earnings (average): $45,950
- Annual earnings (starting): $31,290
- Employed: 182,000
- Growth: 23.2%
- Annual job openings: 17,000

Our sources did not provide separate job openings data for this occupation. The figures for employment and job openings listed here are shared with radiologic technologists.

PREPARING FOR THE JOB

Education/training required: Associate degree.

Programs: Allied health diagnostic, intervention, and treatment professions; medical radiologic technology/science—radiation therapist training; radiologic technology/science—radiographer training.

Knowledge/courses: Medicine and dentistry; clerical practices; psychology; physics; biology; chemistry; personnel and human resources; customer and personal service.

Licensure/certification: Certification available in many states.

WORKING CONDITIONS

Physical: Indoors; radiation; disease or infections; standing; walking and running; using hands on objects, tools, or controls.

Work settings: Hospitals and other health-care facilities.

Other job characteristics: Need to be exact or accurate; repeat same tasks; errors have important consequences; automation.

TOP SKILLS

- Science
- Operation monitoring
- Operation and control
- Service orientation
- Equipment selection
- Negotiation

OTHER FACTS

O*NET Code: 29-2034.02

GOE information: Interest area: 08. Health Science. Work group: 08.06. Medical Technology.

Personality type: Realistic. Realistic occupations frequently involve work activities that include practical, hands-on problems and solutions. They often deal with plants, animals, and real-world materials like wood, tools, and machinery. Many of the occupations require working outside and do not involve a lot of paperwork or working closely with others.

WHERE TO FIND OUT MORE

For information about this career, contact

➤ American Society of Radiologic Technologists, 15000 Central Ave. SE, Albuquerque, NM 87123-3917. Internet: www.asrt.org

For the current list of accredited education programs in radiography, contact

➤ Joint Review Committee on Education in Radiologic Technology, 20 N. Wacker Dr., Suite 2850, Chicago, IL 60606-3182. Internet: www.jrcert.org

Associate Degree

Radiologic Technologists

QUICK LOOK

Take X-rays and Computerized Axial Tomography (CAT or CT) scans or administer non-radioactive materials into patient's bloodstream for diagnostic purposes. Includes technologists who specialize in other modalities, such as computed tomography, ultrasound, and magnetic resonance. Review and evaluate developed X-rays, videotape, or computer-generated information to determine whether images are satisfactory for diagnostic purposes. Use radiation safety measures and protection devices to comply with government regulations and to ensure safety of patients and staff. Explain procedures and observe patients to ensure safety and comfort during scans. Operate or oversee operation of radiologic and magnetic imaging equipment to produce images of the body for diagnostic purposes. Position and immobilize patients on the examining table. Position imaging equipment and adjust controls to set exposure time and distance according to the specification of the examination. Key commands and data into a computer to document and specify scan sequences, adjust transmitters and receivers, or photograph certain images. Monitor video display of area being scanned and adjust density or contrast to improve picture quality. Monitor patients' conditions and reactions, reporting abnormal signs to the physician. Prepare and administer oral or injected contrast media to patients. Set up examination rooms, ensuring that all necessary equipment is ready. Take thorough and accurate patient medical histories. Remove and process film. Record, process, and maintain patient data and treatment records and prepare

EYE OPENERS

Although hospitals will remain the primary employer for radiologic technologists, a greater number of new jobs will be found in physicians' offices and diagnostic imaging centers.

- Annual earnings (average): $45,950
- Annual earnings (starting): $31,290
- Employed: 182,000
- Growth: 23.2%
- Annual job openings: 17,000

Our sources did not provide separate job openings data for this occupation. The figures for employment and job openings listed here are shared with radiologic technicians.

reports. Coordinate work with clerical personnel or other technologists. Demonstrate new equipment, procedures, and techniques to staff and provide technical assistance. Provide assistance in dressing or changing seriously ill, injured, or disabled patients. Move ultrasound scanner over a patient's body and watch the pattern produced on the video screen. Measure the thickness of the section to be radiographed, using instruments similar to measuring tapes. Operate fluoroscope to aid the physician in viewing and guiding the wire or catheter through blood vessels to the area of interest. Assign duties to radiologic staff to maintain patient flows and achieve production goals. Collaborate with other medical team members, such as physicians and nurses, to conduct angiography or special vascular procedures. Perform administrative duties, such as developing departmental operating budget, coordinating purchases of supplies and equipment, and preparing work schedules.

PREPARING FOR THE JOB

Education/training required: Associate degree.

Programs: Allied health diagnostic, intervention, and treatment professions; medical radiologic technology/science—radiation therapist training; radiologic technology/science—radiographer training.

Knowledge/courses: Medicine and dentistry; biology; physics; psychology; chemistry; customer and personal service; computers and electronics; English language.

Licensure/certification: Certification available in many states.

WORKING CONDITIONS

Physical: Indoors; disease or infections; standing; walking and running; using hands on objects, tools, or controls; repetitive motions.

Work settings: Hospitals and other health-care facilities.

Other job characteristics: Need to be exact or accurate; repeat same tasks; errors have important consequences.

TOP SKILLS

- Operation monitoring
- Social perceptiveness
- Instructing
- Reading comprehension
- Service orientation
- Active listening

OTHER FACTS

O*NET code: 29-2034.01

GOE information: Interest area: 08. Health Science. Work group: 08.06. Medical Technology.

Personality type: Realistic. Realistic occupations frequently involve work activities that include practical, hands-on problems and solutions. They often deal with plants, animals, and real-world materials like wood, tools, and machinery. Many of the occupations require working outside and do not involve a lot of paperwork or working closely with others.

WHERE TO FIND OUT MORE

For career information, contact

➤ American Society of Radiologic Technologists, 15000 Central Ave. SE, Albuquerque, NM 87123-3917. Internet: www.asrt.org

For the current list of accredited education programs in radiography, contact

➤ Joint Review Committee on Education in Radiologic Technology, 20 N. Wacker Dr., Suite 2850, Chicago, IL 60606-3182. Internet: www.jrcert.org

Associate Degree

Registered Nurses

QUICK LOOK

Assess patient health problems and needs, develop and implement nursing care plans, and maintain medical records. Administer nursing care to ill, injured, convalescent, or disabled patients. May advise patients on health maintenance and disease prevention or provide case management. Maintain accurate, detailed reports and records. Monitor, record, and report symptoms and changes in patients' conditions. Record patients' medical information and vital signs. Modify patient treatment plans as indicated by patients' responses and conditions. Consult and coordinate with health-care team members to assess, plan, implement, and evaluate patient care plans. Order, interpret, and evaluate diagnostic tests to identify and assess patient's condition. Monitor all aspects of patient care, including diet and physical activity.

— EYE OPENERS —

This occupation includes advance practice nurses, such as nurse practitioners, clinical nurse specialists, certified nurse midwives, and certified registered nurse anesthetists. Advanced practice nursing is practiced by registered nurses who have specialized formal, post-basic education and who function in highly autonomous and specialized roles.

- Annual earnings (average): $54,670
- Annual earnings (starting): $38,660
- Employed: 2,394,000
- Growth: 29.4%
- Annual job openings: 229,000

Direct and supervise less-skilled nursing or other health-care personnel or supervise a particular unit. Prepare patients for and assist with examinations and treatments. Observe nurses and visit patients to ensure proper nursing care. Assess the needs of individuals, families, or communities, including assessment of individuals' home or work environments, to identify potential health or safety problems. Instruct individuals, families, and other groups on topics such as health education, disease prevention, and childbirth. Develop health improvement programs. Prepare rooms, sterile instruments, equipment, and supplies and ensure that stock of supplies is maintained. Inform physicians of a patient's condition during anesthesia. Deliver infants and provide prenatal and postpartum care and treatment under an obstetrician's supervision. Administer local, inhalation, intravenous, and other anesthetics. Provide health care, first aid, immunizations, and assistance in convalescence and rehabilitation in locations such as schools, hospitals, and workplaces. Conduct specified laboratory tests. Perform physical examinations, make tentative diagnoses, and treat patients en route to hospitals or at disaster site triage centers. Hand items to surgeons during operations. Prescribe or recommend drugs; medical devices; or other forms of treatment, such as physical therapy, inhalation therapy, or related therapeutic procedures. Direct and coordinate infection control programs, advising and consulting with specified personnel about necessary precautions. Perform administrative and managerial functions, such as taking responsibility for a unit's staff, budget, planning, and long-range goals.

Preparing for the Job

Education/training required: Associate degree.

Programs: Adult health nurse training/nursing; clinical nurse specialist training; critical care nursing; nurse practitioner training; maternal/child health and neonatal nursing; nurse anesthetist training; nursing midwifery; nursing/registered nurse training (RN, ASN, BSN, MSN); nursing science (MS, PhD); occupational and environmental health nursing; pediatric nursing; perioperative/operating room and surgical nurse training/nursing; psychiatric/mental health nurse training/nursing; and public health/community nurse training/nursing.

Knowledge/Courses: Medicine and dentistry; psychology; therapy and counseling; biology; sociology and anthropology; philosophy and theology; customer and personal service; chemistry.

Licensure/certification: Licensure required; certification available for certain specializations.

Working Conditions

Physical: Indoors; noisy; contaminants; disease or infections; standing; using hands on objects, tools, or controls.

Work settings: Hospitals and other health-care facilities, patients' homes, schools, community centers, and offices.

TOP SKILLS

- Social perceptiveness
- Service orientation
- Science
- Time management
- Monitoring
- Instructing

Other job characteristics: Need to be exact or accurate; errors have important consequences; repeat same tasks.

Other Facts

O*NET Code: 29-1111.00

GOE information: Interest area: 08. Health Science. Work group: 08.02. Medicine and Surgery.

Personality type: Social. Social occupations frequently involve working with, communicating with, and teaching people. These occupations often involve helping or providing service to others.

Where to Find Out More

For information on a career as a registered nurse and nursing education, contact

➤ National League for Nursing, 61 Broadway, 33rd Floor, New York, NY 10006. Internet: www.nln.org

➤ American Association of Colleges of Nursing, 1 Dupont Circle NW, Suite 530, Washington, DC 20036. Internet: www.aacn.nche.edu

➤ American Nurses Association, 8515 Georgia Ave., Suite 400, Silver Spring, MD 20910. Internet: nursingworld.org

Respiratory Therapists

QUICK LOOK

Assess, treat, and care for patients with breathing disorders. Assume primary responsibility for all respiratory care modalities, including the supervision of respiratory therapy technicians. Initiate and conduct therapeutic procedures; maintain patient records; and select, assemble, check, and operate equipment. Set up and operate devices such as mechanical ventilators, therapeutic gas administration apparatus, environmental control systems, and aerosol generators, following specified parameters of treatment. Provide emergency care, including artificial respiration, external cardiac massage, and assistance with cardiopulmonary resuscitation. Determine requirements for treatment, such as type, method, and duration of therapy; precautions to be taken; and medication and dosages, that are compatible with physicians' orders. Monitor patient's physiological responses to therapy, such as vital signs, arterial blood gases, and blood chemistry changes, and consult with a physician if adverse reactions occur. Read prescription, measure arterial blood gases, and review patient information to assess a patient's condition. Work as part of a team of physicians, nurses, and other health-care professionals to manage patient care. Enforce safety rules and ensure careful adherence to physicians' orders. Maintain charts that contain patients' pertinent identification and therapy information. Inspect, clean, test, and maintain respiratory therapy equipment to ensure equipment is functioning safely and efficiently, ordering repairs when necessary. Educate patients and their families about their conditions and teach appropriate disease management techniques, such as breathing exercises and the use of medications and respiratory equipment. Explain treatment procedures to patients to gain cooperation and allay fears. Relay blood analysis results to a physician. Perform pulmonary function and adjust equipment to obtain optimum results in therapy. Perform bronchopulmonary drainage and assist or instruct patients in performance of breathing exercises. Demonstrate respiratory care procedures to trainees and other health-care personnel. Teach, train, and supervise students, respiratory therapy technicians, and assistants. Make emergency visits to resolve equipment problems. Use a variety of testing techniques to assist doctors in cardiac and pulmonary research and to diagnose disorders. Conduct tests, such as electrocardiograms (EKGs), stress testing, and lung capacity tests, to evaluate patients' cardiopulmonary functions.

── EYE OPENERS ──

Almost all states require respiratory therapists to obtain a license.

- Annual earnings (average): $45,140
- Annual earnings (starting): $33,680
- Employed: 94,000
- Growth: 28.4%
- Annual job openings: 7,000

PREPARING FOR THE JOB

Education/training required: Associate degree.

Programs: Respiratory care therapy/therapist training.

Knowledge/courses: Medicine and dentistry; biology; psychology; customer and personal service; therapy and counseling; chemistry; education and training; philosophy and theology.

Licensure/certification: Licensure required in almost all states.

WORKING CONDITIONS

Physical: Indoors; disease or infections; standing.

Work settings: Hospitals and other health-care facilities and patients' homes.

Other job characteristics: Need to be exact or accurate; errors have important consequences.

OTHER FACTS

O*NET code: 29-1126.00

GOE information: Interest area: 08. Health Science. Work group: 08.07. Medical Therapy.

Personality type: Investigative. Investigative occupations frequently involve working with ideas and require an extensive amount of thinking. These occupations can involve searching for facts and figuring out problems.

TOP SKILLS

- Science
- Operation monitoring
- Mathematics
- Instructing
- Active learning
- Reading comprehension

WHERE TO FIND OUT MORE

Information concerning a career in respiratory care is available from

➤ American Association for Respiratory Care, 9425 N. MacArthur Blvd., Suite 100, Irving, TX 75063-4706. Internet: www.aarc.org

For a list of accredited educational programs for respiratory care practitioners, contact the following organization:

➤ Commission on Accreditation for Allied Health Education Programs, 1361 Park St., Clearwater, FL 33756. Internet: www.caahep.org

Associate Degree

Veterinary Technologists and Technicians

QUICK LOOK

Perform medical tests in a laboratory environment for use in the treatment and diagnosis of diseases in animals. Prepare vaccines and serums for prevention of diseases. Prepare tissue samples, take blood samples, and execute laboratory tests, such as urinalysis and blood counts. Clean and sterilize instruments and materials and maintain equipment and machines. Under the direction of a veterinarian, administer anesthesia to animals and monitor their responses to anesthetics so that dosages can be adjusted. Care for and monitor the condition of animals recovering from surgery. Prepare and administer medications, vaccines, serums, and treatments as prescribed by veterinarians. Perform laboratory tests on blood, urine, and feces, such as urinalyses and blood counts, to assist in the diagnosis and treatment of animal health problems. Administer emergency first aid, such as performing emergency resuscitation or other life-saving procedures. Collect, prepare, and label samples for laboratory testing, culture, or microscopic examination. Clean and sterilize instruments, equipment, and materials. Provide veterinarians with the correct equipment and instruments as needed. Fill prescriptions, measuring medications and labeling containers. Prepare animals for surgery, performing such tasks as shaving surgical areas. Take animals into treatment areas and assist with physical examinations by performing such duties as obtaining temperature, pulse, and respiration data. Observe the behavior and condition of animals and monitor their clinical symptoms. Take and develop diagnostic radiographs, using X-ray equipment. Maintain laboratory, research, and treatment records, as well as inventories of pharmaceuticals, equipment, and supplies. Give enemas and perform catheterizations, ear flushes, intravenous feedings, and gavages. Prepare treatment rooms for surgery. Maintain instruments, equipment, and machinery to ensure proper working condition. Perform dental work such as cleaning, polishing, and extracting teeth. Clean kennels, animal holding areas, surgery suites, examination rooms, and animal loading/unloading facilities to control the spread of disease. Provide information and counseling regarding issues such as animal health care, behavior problems, and nutrition. Provide assistance with animal euthanasia and the disposal of remains. Dress and suture wounds and apply splints and other protective devices. Perform a variety of office, clerical, and accounting duties, such as reception, billing, bookkeeping, or selling products.

EYE OPENERS

Keen competition is expected for jobs in zoos.

- Annual earnings (average): $25,670
- Annual earnings (starting): $17,700
- Employed: 60,000
- Growth: 35.3%
- Annual job openings: 9,000

PREPARING FOR THE JOB

Education/training required: Associate degree.

Programs: Veterinary/animal health technology/technician and veterinary assistant training.

Knowledge/courses: Biology; medicine and dentistry; chemistry; sales and marketing; customer and personal service; mathematics; therapy and counseling; clerical practices.

Licensure/certification: Certification available; certification or licensure required in some states.

WORKING CONDITIONS

Physical: Indoors; contaminants; radiation; disease or infections; minor burns, cuts, bites, or stings; standing.

Work settings: Offices, kennels, farms, laboratories, or meat-processing plants.

Other job characteristics: Errors have important consequences; need to be exact or accurate; repeat same tasks.

OTHER FACTS

O*NET Code: 29-2056.00

GOE information: Interest area: 08. Health Science. Work group: 08.05. Animal Care.

Personality type: No data available.

TOP SKILLS

- Science
- Operation monitoring
- Instructing
- Equipment maintenance
- Social perceptiveness
- Operation and control

Associate Degree

WHERE TO FIND OUT MORE

For information on careers in veterinary medicine and a listing of accredited veterinary technology programs, contact

➤ American Veterinary Medical Association, 1931 N. Meacham Rd., Suite 100, Schaumburg, IL 60173-4360. Internet: www.avma.org

QUICK LOOK

Evaluate, advise, and treat athletes to assist recovery from injury, avoid injury, or maintain peak physical fitness. Conduct an initial assessment of an athlete's injury or illness to provide emergency or continued care and to determine whether the athlete should be referred to physicians for definitive diagnosis and treatment. Care for athletic injuries, using physical therapy equipment, techniques, and medication. Evaluate athletes' readiness to play and provide participation clearances when necessary and warranted. Apply protective or injury preventive devices such as tape, bandages, or braces to body parts such as ankles, fingers, or wrists. Assess and report the progress of recovering athletes to coaches and physicians. Collaborate with physicians to develop and implement comprehensive rehabilitation programs for athletic injuries. Advise athletes on the proper use of equipment. Plan and implement comprehensive athletic injury and illness prevention programs. Develop training programs and routines designed to improve athletic performance. Travel with athletic teams to be available at sporting events. Instruct coaches, athletes, parents, medical personnel, and community members in the care and prevention of athletic injuries. Inspect playing fields to locate any items that could injure players. Conduct research and provide instruction on subject matter related to athletic training or sports medicine. Recommend special diets to improve athletes' health, increase their stamina, or alter their weight. Massage body parts to relieve soreness, strains, and bruises. Confer with coaches to select protective equipment. Accompany injured athletes to hospitals. Perform team-support duties, such as running errands, maintaining equipment, and stocking supplies. Lead stretching exercises for team members prior to games and practices.

EYE OPENERS

About 7 out of 10 athletic trainers have a master's or higher degree.

- Annual earnings (average): $34,260
- Annual earnings (starting): $20,240
- Employed: 15,000
- Growth: 29.3%
- Annual job openings: 1,000

PREPARING FOR THE JOB

Education/training required: Bachelor's degree.

Programs: Athletic training/trainer training.

Knowledge/courses: Therapy and counseling; medicine and dentistry; biology; psychology; sociology and anthropology; education and training; customer and personal service; physics.

Licensure/certification: Certification available; licensure required in some states.

WORKING CONDITIONS

Physical: More often indoors than outdoors; very hot or cold; contaminants; disease or infections; standing.

Work settings: Offices, hospitals, clinics, colleges, or stadiums.

Other job characteristics: Need to be exact or accurate; errors have important consequences.

OTHER FACTS

O*NET code: 29-9091.00

GOE information: Interest area: 08. Health Science. Work group: 08.09. Health Protection and Promotion.

TOP SKILLS

- Social perceptiveness
- Science
- Management of material resources
- Management of financial resources
- Time management
- Management of personnel resources

Personality type: Social. Social occupations frequently involve working with, communicating with, and teaching people. These occupations often involve helping or providing service to others.

WHERE TO FIND OUT MORE

For further information on careers in athletic training, contact

➤ National Athletic Trainers' Association, 2952 Stemmons Freeway, Dallas, TX 75247. Internet: www.nata.org

For information on certification, contact

➤ Board of Certification, Inc., 4223 S. 143rd Circle, Omaha, NE 68137. Internet: www.bocatc.org

Bachelor's Degree

Biomedical Engineers

QUICK LOOK

Apply knowledge of engineering, biology, and biomechanical principles to the design, development, and evaluation of biological and health systems and products, such as artificial organs, prostheses, instrumentation, medical information systems, and health management and care delivery systems. Evaluate the safety, efficiency, and effectiveness of biomedical equipment. Install, adjust, maintain, and/or repair biomedical equipment. Advise hospital administrators on the planning, acquisition, and use of medical equipment. Advise and assist in the application of instrumentation in clinical environments. Develop models or computer simulations of human bio-behavioral systems in order to obtain data for measuring or controlling life processes. Research new materials to be used for products such as implanted artificial organs. Design and develop medical diagnostic and clinical instrumentation, equipment, and procedures, utilizing the principles of engineering and bio-behavioral sciences. Conduct research with life scientists, chemists, and medical scientists on the engineering aspects of the biological systems of humans and animals. Teach biomedical engineering or disseminate knowledge about field through writing or consulting. Design and deliver technology to assist people with disabilities. Diagnose and interpret bio-electric data, using signal-processing techniques. Adapt or design computer hardware or software for medical science uses. Analyze new medical procedures in order to forecast likely outcomes. Develop new applications for energy sources, such as using nuclear power for biomedical implants.

— EYE OPENERS —

Biomedical engineering has the highest percentage of female students in all of the engineering specialties.

- Annual earnings (average): $71,840
- Annual earnings (starting): $44,060
- Employed: 10,000
- Growth: 30.7%
- Annual job openings: 1,000

PREPARING FOR THE JOB

Education/training required: Bachelor's degree.

Programs: Biomedical/medical engineering.

Knowledge/courses: Engineering and technology; computers and electronics; physics; design; mechanical devices; chemistry; biology; medicine and dentistry.

Licensure/certification: Licensure required for engineers who offer their services directly to the public; certification available.

WORKING CONDITIONS

Physical: Indoors; contaminants; disease or infections; hazardous conditions; sitting; using hands on objects, tools, or controls.

Work settings: Mostly office buildings, laboratories, or industrial plants.

Other job characteristics: Need to be exact or accurate; errors have important consequences; repeat same tasks.

```
┌──────── TOP SKILLS ────────┐
│                            │
│  • Technology design       │
│  • Science                 │
│  • Installation            │
│  • Operations analysis     │
│  • Quality control analysis│
│  • Systems evaluation      │
│                            │
└────────────────────────────┘
```

OTHER FACTS

O*NET code: 17-2031.00

GOE information: Interest area: 15. Scientific Research, Engineering, and Mathematics. Work group: 15.07. Research and Design Engineering.

Personality type: No data available.

WHERE TO FIND OUT MORE

Information about careers in engineering is available from

➤ JETS (Junior Engineering Technical Society), 1420 King St., Suite 405, Alexandria, VA 22314-2794. Internet: www.jets.org

Information on accredited engineering programs is available from

➤ ABET(Accreditation Board for Engineering and Technology, Inc.), 111 Market Place, Suite 1050, Baltimore, MD 21202-4012. Internet: www.abet.org

Bachelor's Degree

QUICK LOOK

Plan and conduct food service or nutritional programs to assist in the promotion of health and control of disease. May supervise activities of a department providing quantity food services, counsel individuals, or conduct nutritional research. Assess nutritional needs, diet restrictions, and current health plans to develop and implement dietary-care plans and provide nutritional counseling. Consult with physicians and health-care personnel to determine nutritional needs and diet restrictions of patient or client. Advise patients and their families on nutritional principles, dietary plans and diet modifications, and food selection and preparation. Counsel individuals and groups on the basic rules of good nutrition, healthy eating habits, and nutrition monitoring to improve their quality of life. Monitor food service operations to ensure conformance to nutritional, safety, sanitation, and quality standards. Coordinate recipe development and standardization and develop new menus for independent food service operations. Develop policies for food service or nutritional programs to promote health and control disease. Inspect meals served for conformance to prescribed diets and standards of palatability and appearance. Develop curriculum and prepare manuals, visual aids, course outlines, and other materials used in teaching. Prepare and administer budgets for food, equipment, and supplies. Purchase food in accordance with health and safety codes. Select, train, and supervise workers who plan, prepare, and serve meals. Manage quantity food service departments or clinical and community nutrition services. Coordinate diet counseling services. Advise food service managers and organizations on sanitation, safety procedures, menu development, budgeting, and planning to assist with the establishment, operation, and evaluation of food service facilities and nutrition programs. Organize, develop, analyze, test, and prepare special meals such as low-fat, low-cholesterol, and chemical-free meals. Plan, conduct, and evaluate dietary, nutritional, and epidemiological research. Plan and conduct training programs in dietetics, nutrition, and institutional management and administration for medical students, health-care personnel, and the general public. Make recommendations regarding public policy, such as nutrition labeling, food fortification, and nutrition standards for school programs.

EYE OPENERS

Most jobs for dietitians and nutritionists are in hospitals, nursing care facilities, and offices of physicians or other health practitioners.

- Annual earnings (average): $44,940
- Annual earnings (starting): $29,050
- Employed: 50,000
- Growth: 18.3%
- Annual job openings: 4,000

PREPARING FOR THE JOB

Education/training required: Bachelor's degree.

Programs: Clinical nutrition/nutritionist training; dietetics and clinical nutrition services; dietetics/dietitian (RD); foods, nutrition, and related services; foods, nutrition, and wellness studies; foodservice systems administration/management; human nutrition; nutrition sciences.

Knowledge/courses: Food production; therapy and counseling; sociology and anthropology; medicine and dentistry; philosophy and theology; psychology; education and training; chemistry.

Licensure/certification: Licensure or certification generally required.

WORKING CONDITIONS

Physical: Indoors; more often sitting than standing.

Work settings: Usually offices; sometimes kitchens.

Other job characteristics: Need to be exact or accurate.

OTHER FACTS

O*NET code: 29-1031.00

GOE information: Interest area: 08. Health Science. Work group: 08.09. Health Protection and Promotion.

Personality type: Investigative. Investigative occupations frequently involve working with ideas and require an extensive amount of thinking. These occupations can involve searching for facts and figuring out problems.

TOP SKILLS

- Science
- Social perceptiveness
- Writing
- Instructing
- Speaking
- Reading comprehension

WHERE TO FIND OUT MORE

For a list of academic programs, scholarships, and other information about dietetics, contact

➤ American Dietetic Association, 120 S. Riverside Plaza, Suite 2000, Chicago, IL 60606-6995. Internet: www.eatright.org

Bachelor's Degree

QUICK LOOK

Plan, implement, and coordinate safety programs, which require the application of engineering principles and technology, in order to prevent or correct unsafe environmental working conditions. Investigate industrial accidents, injuries, or occupational diseases to determine causes and preventive measures. Report or review findings from accident investigations, facilities inspections, or environmental testing. Maintain and apply knowledge of current policies, regulations, and industrial processes. Inspect facilities, machinery, and safety equipment to identify and correct potential hazards and to ensure safety regulation compliance. Conduct or coordinate worker training in areas such as safety laws and regulations, hazardous condition monitoring, and use of safety equipment. Review employee safety programs to determine their adequacy. Interview employers and employees to obtain information about work environments and workplace incidents. Review plans and specifications for construction of new machinery or equipment to determine whether all safety requirements have been met. Compile, analyze, and interpret statistical data related to occupational illnesses and accidents. Interpret safety regulations for others interested in industrial safety, such as safety engineers, labor representatives, and safety inspectors. Recommend process and product safety features that will reduce employees' exposure to chemical, physical, and biological work hazards. Conduct or direct testing of air quality, noise, temperature, or radiation levels to verify compliance with health and safety regulations. Provide technical advice and guidance to organizations on how to handle health-related problems and make needed changes. Confer with medical professionals to assess health risks and to develop ways to manage health issues and concerns. Install safety devices on machinery or direct device installation. Maintain liaisons with outside organizations such as fire departments, mutual aid societies, and rescue teams in order to facilitate emergency responses. Evaluate adequacy of actions taken to correct health inspection violations. Write and revise safety regulations and codes. Check floors of plants to ensure that they are strong enough to support heavy machinery. Plan and conduct industrial hygiene research.

EYE OPENERS

Continuing education is critical for engineers wishing to enhance their value to employers as technology evolves.

- Annual earnings (average): $65,210
- Annual earnings (starting): $40,230
- Employed: 27,000
- Growth: 13.4%
- Annual job openings: 2,000

Our sources did not provide separate job openings data for this occupation. The figures for employment and job openings listed here are shared with fire-prevention and protection engineers and with product safety engineers.

PREPARING FOR THE JOB

Education/training required: Bachelor's degree.

Programs: Environmental/health engineering.

Knowledge/courses: Building and construction; education and training; chemistry; physics; engineering and technology; biology; public safety and security; personnel and human resources.

Licensure/certification: Licensure required for engineers who offer their services directly to the public; certification available.

WORKING CONDITIONS

Physical: More often indoors than outdoors; noisy; sitting.

Work settings: Mostly office buildings, laboratories, or industrial plants. May travel to plants or worksites.

Other job characteristics: Need to be exact or accurate; errors have important consequences.

TOP SKILLS

- Management of financial resources
- Science
- Systems analysis
- Persuasion
- Systems evaluation
- Management of personnel resources

OTHER FACTS

O*NET code: 17-2111.01

GOE information: Interest area: 15. Scientific Research, Engineering, and Mathematics. Work group: 15.08. Industrial and Safety Engineering.

Personality type: Investigative. Investigative occupations frequently involve working with ideas and require an extensive amount of thinking. These occupations can involve searching for facts and figuring out problems.

WHERE TO FIND OUT MORE

Information about careers in engineering is available from

> ➤ JETS (Junior Engineering Technical Society), 1420 King St., Suite 405, Alexandria, VA 22314-2794. Internet: www.jets.org

Information on accredited engineering programs is available from

> ➤ ABET (Accreditation Board for Engineering and Technology, Inc.), 111 Market Place, Suite 1050, Baltimore, MD 21202-4012. Internet: www.abet.org

Bachelor's Degree

Medical and Clinical Laboratory Technologists

QUICK LOOK

Perform complex medical laboratory tests for diagnosis, treatment, and prevention of disease. May train or supervise staff. Analyze laboratory findings to check the accuracy of the results. Conduct chemical analysis of body fluids, including blood, urine, and spinal fluid, to determine presence of normal and abnormal components. Operate, calibrate, and maintain equipment used in quantitative and qualitative analysis, such as spectrophotometers, calorimeters, flame photometers, and computer-controlled analyzers. Enter data from analysis of medical tests and clinical results into computer for storage. Analyze samples of biological material for chemical content or reaction. Establish and monitor programs to ensure the accuracy of laboratory results. Set up, clean, and maintain laboratory equipment. Provide technical information about test results to physicians, family members, and researchers. Supervise, train, and direct lab assistants, medical and clinical laboratory technicians and technologists, and other medical laboratory workers engaged in laboratory testing. Develop, standardize, evaluate, and modify procedures, techniques, and tests used in the analysis of specimens and in medical laboratory experiments. Cultivate, isolate, and assist in identifying microbial organisms and perform various tests on these microorganisms. Study blood samples to determine the number of cells and their morphology, as well as the blood group, type, and compatibility for transfusion purposes, using microscopic technique. Obtain, cut, stain, and mount biological material on slides for microscopic study and diagnosis, following standard laboratory procedures. Select and prepare specimen and media for cell culture, using aseptic technique and knowledge of medium components and cell requirements. Conduct medical research under direction of a microbiologist or biochemist. Harvest cell cultures at optimum time based on knowledge of cell cycle differences and culture conditions.

EYE OPENERS

Clinical laboratory technologists usually have a bachelor's degree with a major in medical technology or in one of the life sciences.

- Annual earnings (average): $47,710
- Annual earnings (starting): $33,480
- Employed: 156,000
- Growth: 20.5%
- Annual job openings: 14,000

Preparing for the Job

Education/training required: Bachelor's degree.

Programs: Clinical laboratory science/medical technology/technologist training; clinical/medical laboratory science and allied professions, other; cytogenetics/genetics/clinical genetics technology/technologist training; cytotechnology/cytotechnologist training; histologic technology/histotechnologist training; renal/dialysis technologist/technician training.

Knowledge/courses: Biology; chemistry; mechanical devices; public safety and security; computers and electronics; medicine and dentistry; mathematics; English language.

Licensure/certification: Certification available; licensure required in some states.

Working Conditions

Physical: Indoors; contaminants; disease or infections; hazardous conditions; using hands on objects, tools, or controls; repetitive motions.

Work settings: Laboratories in large hospitals or independent laboratories.

Other job characteristics: Need to be exact or accurate; repeat same tasks; errors have important consequences; automation; pace determined by speed of equipment.

TOP SKILLS

- Equipment maintenance
- Operation monitoring
- Quality control analysis
- Science
- Operation and control
- Repairing

Other Facts

O*NET code: 29-2011.00

GOE information: Interest area: 08. Health Science. Work group: 08.06. Medical Technology.

Personality type: Investigative. Investigative occupations frequently involve working with ideas and require an extensive amount of thinking. These occupations can involve searching for facts and figuring out problems.

Where to Find Out More

For information on accredited programs and certification, contact

➤ National Accrediting Agency for Clinical Laboratory Sciences, 8410 W. Bryn Mawr Ave., Suite 670, Chicago, IL 60631. Internet: www.naacls.org

➤ American Association of Bioanalysts, Board of Registry, 906 Olive St., Suite 1200, St. Louis, MO 63101-1434. Internet: www.aab.org

➤ American Medical Technologists, 10700 W. Higgins Rd., Rosemont, IL 60018. Internet: www.amt1.com

➤ American Society for Clinical Pathology, 33 W. Monroe, Suite 1600, Chicago, IL 60603. Internet: www.ascp.org

Bachelor's Degree

Medical and Public Health Social Workers

QUICK LOOK

Provide persons, families, or vulnerable populations with the psychosocial support needed to cope with chronic, acute, or terminal illnesses, such as Alzheimer's, cancer, or AIDS. Services include advising family caregivers, providing patient education and counseling, and making necessary referrals for other social services. Collaborate with other professionals to evaluate patients' medical or physical condition and to assess client needs. Investigate child abuse or neglect cases and take authorized protective action when necessary. Refer patient, client, or family to community resources to assist in recovery from mental or physical illness and to provide access to services such as financial assistance, legal aid, housing, job placement, or education. Counsel clients and patients in individual and group sessions to help them overcome dependencies, recover from illness, and adjust to life. Organize support groups or counsel family members to assist them in understanding, dealing with, and supporting the client or patient. Advocate for clients or patients to resolve crises. Identify environmental impediments to client or patient progress through interviews and review of patient records. Utilize consultation data and social work experience to plan and coordinate client or patient care and rehabilitation, following through to ensure service efficacy. Modify treatment plans to comply with changes in clients' status. Monitor, evaluate, and record client progress according to measurable goals described in treatment and care plan. Supervise and direct other workers providing services to clients or patients. Develop or advise on social policy and assist in community development. Oversee Medicaid- and Medicare-related paperwork and recordkeeping in hospitals. Conduct social research to advance knowledge in the social work field. Plan and conduct programs to combat social problems, prevent substance abuse, or improve community health and counseling services.

— EYE OPENERS —

Although a bachelor's degree is the minimum requirement for medical and public health social workers, a master's degree in social work or a related field has become the standard for many positions.

- Annual earnings (average): $41,120
- Annual earnings (starting): $26,130
- Employed: 110,000
- Growth: 25.9%
- Annual job openings: 14,000

PREPARING FOR THE JOB

Education/training required: Bachelor's degree.

Programs: Clinical/medical social work.

Knowledge/courses: Therapy and counseling; psychology; philosophy and theology; sociology and anthropology; medicine and dentistry; customer and personal service; education and training; law and government.

Licensure/certification: Licensing, certification, or registration required.

WORKING CONDITIONS

Physical: Indoors; noisy; disease or infections; sitting.

Work settings: Usually offices or residential facilities, but sometimes homes of clients or offices of service providers.

Other job characteristics: Need to be exact or accurate.

OTHER FACTS

O*NET code: 21-1022.00

GOE information: Interest area: 10. Human Service. Work group: 10.01. Counseling and Social Work.

Personality type: Social. Social occupations frequently involve working with, communicating with, and teaching people. These occupations often involve helping or providing service to others.

TOP SKILLS

- Social perceptiveness
- Service orientation
- Negotiation
- Coordination
- Active listening
- Speaking

WHERE TO FIND OUT MORE

For information about career opportunities in social work and voluntary credentials for social workers, contact

➤ National Association of Social Workers, 750 First St. NE, Suite 700, Washington, DC 20002-4241. Internet: www.socialworkers.org

For a listing of accredited social work programs, contact

➤ Council on Social Work Education, 1725 Duke St., Suite 500, Alexandria, VA 22314-3457. Internet: www.cswe.org

Bachelor's Degree

QUICK LOOK

Assist patients who have disabling conditions of limbs and spine or partial or total absence of limb by fitting and preparing orthopedic braces or prostheses. Examine, interview, and measure patients in order to determine their appliance needs and to identify factors that could affect appliance fit. Fit, test, and evaluate devices on patients and make adjustments for proper fit, function, and comfort. Instruct patients in the use and care of orthoses and prostheses. Design orthopedic and prosthetic devices based on physicians' prescriptions and examination and measurement of patients. Maintain patients' records. Make and modify plaster casts of areas that will be fitted with prostheses or orthoses for use in the device construction process. Select materials and components to be used, based on device design. Confer with physicians to formulate specifications and prescriptions for orthopedic or prosthetic devices. Repair, rebuild, and modify prosthetic and orthopedic appliances. Construct and fabricate appliances or supervise others who are constructing the appliances. Train and supervise orthopedic and prosthetic assistants and technicians and other support staff. Update skills and knowledge by attending conferences and seminars. Show and explain orthopedic and prosthetic appliances to health-care workers. Research new ways to construct and use orthopedic and prosthetic devices. Publish research findings and present them at conferences and seminars.

EYE OPENERS

Because the number of job openings for orthotists and prothetists is expected to exceed the number of practitioners, job opportunities will be excellent.

- Annual earnings (average): $53,760
- Annual earnings (starting): $29,110
- Employed: 6,000
- Growth: 18.0%
- Annual job openings: Fewer than 500

PREPARING FOR THE JOB

Education/training required: Bachelor's degree.

Programs: Assistive/augmentative technology and rehabiliation engineering; orthotist/prosthetist training.

Knowledge/courses: Engineering and technology; medicine and dentistry; design; therapy and counseling; psychology; production and processing; mechanical devices; sales and marketing.

Licensure/certification: Certification available.

WORKING CONDITIONS

Physical: Indoors; noisy; contaminants; disease or infections; hazardous equipment; using hands on objects, tools, or controls.

Work settings: Orthotic and prosthetic fabrication laboratories, hospitals, and other health-care facilities.

Other job characteristics: Need to be exact or accurate; errors have important consequences.

TOP SKILLS

- Technology design
- Management of financial resources
- Management of material resources
- Service orientation
- Management of personnel resources
- Operations analysis

OTHER FACTS

O*NET code: 29-2091.00

GOE information: Interest area: 08. Health Science. Work group: 08.06. Medical Technology.

Personality type: Social. Social occupations frequently involve working with, communicating with, and teaching people. These occupations often involve helping or providing service to others.

WHERE TO FIND OUT MORE

For information on careers in orthotics and prosthetics, contact

➤ American Academy of Orthotists and Prosthetists, 526 King St., Suite 201, Alexandria, VA 22314. Internet: www.opcareers.org

For a list of accredited programs in orthotics and prosthetics, contact

➤ National Commission on Orthotic and Prosthetic Education, 330 John Carlyle St., Suite 200, Alexandria, VA 22314. Internet: www.ncope.org

Bachelor's Degree

Physician Assistants

QUICK LOOK

Provide health-care services typically performed by a physician, under the supervision of a physician. Conduct complete physicals, provide treatment, and counsel patients. May, in some cases, prescribe medication. Must graduate from an accredited educational program for physician assistants. Examine patients to obtain information about their physical condition. Make tentative diagnoses and decisions about management and treatment of patients. Interpret diagnostic test results for deviations from normal. Obtain, compile, and record patient medical data, including health history, progress notes, and results of physical examination. Administer or order diagnostic tests, such as X-ray, electrocardiogram, and laboratory tests. Prescribe therapy or medication with physician approval. Perform therapeutic procedures, such as injections, immunizations, suturing and wound care, and infection management. Instruct and counsel patients about prescribed therapeutic regimens, normal growth and development, family planning, emotional problems of daily living, and health maintenance. Provide physicians with assistance during surgery or complicated medical procedures. Supervise and coordinate activities of technicians and technical assistants. Visit and observe patients on hospital rounds or house calls, updating charts, ordering therapy, and reporting back to physician. Order medical and laboratory supplies and equipment.

EYE OPENERS

Admission requirements vary among physician assistant programs, but many require at least two years of college and some health care experience.

- Annual earnings (average): $72,030
- Annual earnings (starting): $38,370
- Employed: 62,000
- Growth: 49.6%
- Annual job openings: 10,000

PREPARING FOR THE JOB

Education/training required: Bachelor's degree.

Programs: Physician assistant training.

Knowledge/courses: Medicine and dentistry; biology; therapy and counseling; psychology; chemistry; customer and personal service; English language; education and training.

Licensure/certification: Licensure required; certification available for certain specializations.

WORKING CONDITIONS

Physical: Indoors; disease or infections; standing.

Work settings: Physicians' offices and hospitals.

Other job characteristics: Need to be exact or accurate; errors have important consequences.

OTHER FACTS

O*NET code: 29-1071.00

GOE information: Interest area: 08. Health Science. Work group: 08.02. Medicine and Surgery.

Personality type: Investigative. Investigative occupations frequently involve working with ideas and require an extensive amount of thinking. These occupations can involve searching for facts and figuring out problems.

TOP SKILLS

- Science
- Social perceptiveness
- Reading comprehension
- Critical thinking
- Active listening
- Instructing

WHERE TO FIND OUT MORE

For information on a career as a physician assistant, including a list of accredited programs, contact

➤ American Academy of Physician Assistants Information Center, 950 N. Washington St., Alexandria, VA 22314-1552. Internet: www.aapa.org

For eligibility requirements and a description of the Physician Assistant National Certifying Examination, contact

➤ National Commission on Certification of Physician Assistants, Inc., 12000 Findley Rd., Suite 200, Duluth, GA 30097. Internet: www.nccpa.net

Bachelor's Degree

Recreational Therapists

QUICK LOOK

Plan, direct, or coordinate medically approved recreation programs for patients in hospitals, nursing homes, or other institutions. Activities include sports, trips, dramatics, social activities, and arts and crafts. May assess a patient's condition and recommend appropriate recreational activity. Observe, analyze, and record patients' participation, reactions, and progress during treatment sessions, modifying treatment programs as needed. Develop treatment plan to meet needs of patient, based on needs assessment, patient interests, and objectives of therapy. Encourage clients with special needs and circumstances to acquire new skills and get involved in health-promoting leisure activities, such as sports, games, arts and crafts, and gardening. Counsel and encourage patients to develop leisure activities. Confer with members of treatment team to plan and evaluate therapy programs. Conduct therapy sessions to improve patients' mental and physical well-being. Instruct patient in activities and techniques, such as sports, dance, music, art, or relaxation techniques, designed to meet their specific physical or psychological needs. Obtain information from medical records, medical staff, family members, and the patients themselves to assess patients' capabilities, needs, and interests. Plan, organize, direct, and participate in treatment programs and activities to facilitate patients' rehabilitation, help them integrate into the community, and prevent further medical problems. Prepare and submit reports and charts to treatment team to reflect patients' reactions and evidence of progress or regression.

EYE OPENERS

The best job opportunities for recreational therapists should be in community care facilities for the elderly and in residential mental retardation, mental health, and substance abuse facilities.

- Annual earnings (average): $33,480
- Annual earnings (starting): $20,140
- Employed: 24,000
- Growth: 5.7%
- Annual job openings: 3,000

PREPARING FOR THE JOB

Education/training required: Bachelor's degree.

Programs: Therapeutic recreation/recreational therapy.

Knowledge/courses: Psychology; therapy and counseling; fine arts; sociology and anthropology; philosophy and theology; customer and personal service; medicine and dentistry; transportation.

Licensure/certification: Certification available; certification or licensure required in some states.

WORKING CONDITIONS

Physical: Indoors; disease or infections; standing.

Work settings: Special activity rooms, offices, parks, playgrounds, swimming pools, restaurants, and theaters.

Other job characteristics: Need to be exact or accurate; errors have important consequences.

---— TOP SKILLS —---

- Social perceptiveness
- Writing
- Persuasion
- Instructing
- Learning strategies
- Service orientation

OTHER FACTS

O*NET code: 29-1125.00

GOE information: Interest area: 08. Health Science. Work group: 08.07. Medical Therapy.

Personality type: Social. Social occupations frequently involve working with, communicating with, and teaching people. These occupations often involve helping or providing service to others.

WHERE TO FIND OUT MORE

For information on how to order materials describing careers and academic programs in recreational therapy, contact

➤ American Therapeutic Recreation Association, 1414 Prince St., Suite 204, Alexandria, VA 22314-2853. Internet: www.atra-tr.org

➤ National Therapeutic Recreation Society, 22377 Belmont Ridge Rd., Ashburn, VA 20148-4501. Internet: www.nrpa.org/content/default.aspx?documentid=530

Medical and Health Services Managers

QUICK LOOK

Plan, direct, or coordinate medicine and health services in hospitals, clinics, managed care organizations, public health agencies, or similar organizations. Direct, supervise, and evaluate work activities of medical, nursing, technical, clerical, service, maintenance, and other personnel. Establish objectives and evaluative or operational criteria for units. Direct or conduct recruitment, hiring, and training of personnel. Develop and maintain computerized record management systems to store and process data such as personnel activities and information and to produce reports. Develop and implement organizational policies and procedures for the facility or medical unit. Conduct and administer fiscal operations, including accounting, planning budgets, authorizing expenditures, establishing rates for services, and coordinating financial reporting. Establish work schedules and assignments for staff according to workload, space, and equipment availability. Maintain communication between governing boards, medical staff, and department heads by attending board meetings and coordinating interdepartmental functioning. Monitor the use of diagnostic services, inpatient beds, facilities, and staff to ensure effective use of resources and assess the need for additional staff, equipment, and services. Maintain awareness of advances in medicine, computerized diagnostic and treatment equipment, data processing technology, government regulations, health insurance changes, and financing options. Manage change in integrated health-care delivery systems, such as work restructuring, technological innovations, and shifts in the focus of care. Prepare activity reports to inform management of the status and implementation plans of programs, services, and quality initiatives. Plan, implement, and administer programs and services in a health-care or medical facility, including personnel administration, training, and coordination of medical, nursing, and physical plant staff. Consult with medical, business, and community groups to discuss service problems, respond to community needs, enhance public relations, coordinate activities and plans, and promote health programs. Inspect facilities and recommend building or equipment modifications to ensure emergency readiness and compliance with access, safety, and sanitation regulations.

── EYE OPENERS ──

Job applicants with work experience in health care and strong business and management skills likely will have the best opportunities.

- Annual earnings (average): $69,700
- Annual earnings (starting): $43,640
- Employed: 248,000
- Growth: 22.8%
- Annual job openings: 33,000

PREPARING FOR THE JOB

Education/training required: Work experience plus a bachelor's or master's degree.

Programs: Community health and preventive medicine; health and medical administrative services; health information/medical records administration/administrator training; health services administration; health unit manager/ward supervisor training; health/health care administration/management; hospital and health care facilities administration/management; medical staff services technology/technician training; nursing administration (MSN, MS, PhD); public health (MPH, DPH).

Knowledge/courses: Therapy and counseling; medicine and dentistry; philosophy and theology; personnel and human resources; sociology and anthropology; biology; psychology; communications and media.

Licensure/certification: Licensure required for some specializations and in some states.

WORKING CONDITIONS

Physical: Indoors; noisy; disease or infections; sitting.

Work settings: Offices in hospitals, nursing and residential care facilities, and other health-care establishments.

Other job characteristics: Need to be exact or accurate.

TOP SKILLS

- Management of material resources
- Management of personnel resources
- Management of financial resources
- Systems evaluation
- Persuasion
- Service orientation

OTHER FACTS

O*NET code: 11-9111.00

GOE information: Interest area: 08. Health Science. Work group: 08.01. Managerial Work in Medical and Health Services.

Personality type: Enterprising. Enterprising occupations frequently involve starting up and carrying out projects. These occupations can involve leading people and making many decisions. They sometimes require risk taking and often deal with business.

WHERE TO FIND OUT MORE

For information about career opportunities in health-care management, contact

➤ American College of Health Care Administrators, 300 N. Lee St., Suite 301, Alexandria, VA 22314. Internet: www.achca.org

➤ Medical Group Management Association, 104 Inverness Terrace East, Englewood, CO 80112-5306. Internet: www.mgma.org

➤ Professional Association of Health Care Office Management, 461 E. Ten Mile Rd., Pensacola, FL 32534-9712. Internet: www.pahcom.com

Work Experience Plus Degree

QUICK LOOK

Assess and treat persons with hearing and related disorders. May fit hearing aids and provide auditory training. May perform research related to hearing problems. Evaluate hearing and speech/language disorders to determine diagnoses and courses of treatment. Administer hearing or speech/language evaluations, tests, or examinations to patients to collect information on type and degree of impairment, using specialized instruments and electronic equipment. Fit and dispense assistive devices, such as hearing aids. Maintain client records at all stages, including initial evaluation and discharge. Refer clients to additional medical or educational services if needed. Counsel and instruct clients in techniques to improve hearing or speech impairment, including sign language or lip-reading. Monitor clients' progress and discharge them from treatment when goals have been attained. Plan and conduct treatment programs for clients' hearing or speech problems, consulting with physicians, nurses, psychologists, and other health-care personnel as necessary. Recommend assistive devices according to clients' needs or nature of impairments. Participate in conferences or training to update or share knowledge of new hearing or speech disorder treatment methods or technologies. Instruct clients, parents, teachers, or employers in how to avoid behavior patterns that lead to miscommunication. Examine and clean patients' ear canals. Advise educators or other medical staff on speech or hearing topics. Educate and supervise audiology students and health-care personnel. Fit and tune cochlear implants, providing rehabilitation for adjustment to listening with implant amplification systems. Work with multidisciplinary teams to assess and rehabilitate recipients of implanted hearing devices. Develop and supervise hearing screening programs. Conduct or direct research on hearing or speech topics and report findings to help in the development of procedures, technology, or treatments. Measure noise levels in workplaces and conduct hearing protection programs in industry, schools, and communities.

EYE OPENERS

A master's degree in audiology has been the standard credential; however, a clinical doctoral degree is becoming more common.

- Annual earnings (average): $53,490
- Annual earnings (starting): $35,920
- Employed: 10,000
- Growth: 9.1%
- Annual job openings: Fewer than 500

PREPARING FOR THE JOB

Education/training required: Master's degree.

Programs: Audiology/audiologist and speech-language pathology/pathologist training; audiology/audiologist and hearing sciences; communication disorders sciences and services; communication disorders.

Knowledge/courses: Therapy and counseling; medicine and dentistry; psychology; customer and personal service; sales and marketing; English language; sociology and anthropology; computers and electronics.

Licensure/certification: Licensure generally required; certification available.

WORKING CONDITIONS

Physical: Indoors; disease or infections; sitting; using hands on objects, tools, or controls.

Work settings: Offices.

Other job characteristics: Need to be exact or accurate; repeat same tasks.

TOP SKILLS

- Social perceptiveness
- Science
- Service orientation
- Persuasion
- Equipment selection
- Reading comprehension

OTHER FACTS

O*NET code: 29-1121.00

GOE information: Interest area: 08. Health Science. Work group: 08.07. Medical Therapy.

Personality type: Social. Social occupations frequently involve working with, communicating with, and teaching people. These occupations often involve helping or providing service to others.

WHERE TO FIND OUT MORE

General information on careers in audiology is available from

➤ American Academy of Audiology, 11730 Plaza America Dr., Suite 300, Reston, VA 20190. Internet: www.audiology.org

➤ American Speech-Language-Hearing Association, 10801 Rockville Pike, Rockville, MD 20852. Internet: www.asha.org

53 Environmental Scientists and Specialists, Including Health

QUICK LOOK

Conduct research or perform investigation for the purpose of identifying, abating, or eliminating sources of pollutants or hazards that affect either the environment or the health of the population. Utilizing knowledge of various scientific disciplines, may collect, synthesize, study, report, and take action based on data derived from measurements or observations of air, food, soil, water, and other sources. Conduct environmental audits and inspections and investigations of violations. Evaluate violations or problems discovered during inspections to determine appropriate regulatory actions or to provide advice on the development and prosecution of regulatory cases. Communicate scientific and technical information through oral briefings, written documents, workshops, conferences, and public hearings. Review and implement environmental technical standards, guidelines, policies, and formal regulations. Provide technical guidance, support, and oversight to environmental programs, industry, and the public. Provide advice on proper standards and regulations or the development of policies, strategies, and codes of practice for environmental management. Analyze data to determine validity, quality, and scientific significance and to interpret correlations between human activities and environmental effects. Collect, synthesize, and analyze data derived from pollution emission measurements, atmospheric monitoring, meteorological and mineralogical information, and soil or water samples. Determine data collection methods to be employed in research projects and surveys. Prepare charts or graphs from data samples, providing summary information on the environmental relevance of the data. Develop the technical portions of legal documents, administrative orders, or consent decrees. Investigate and report on accidents affecting the environment. Monitor environmental impacts of development activities. Supervise environmental technologists and technicians. Develop programs designed to obtain the most productive, nondamaging use of land. Research sources of pollution to determine their effects on the environment and to develop theories or methods of pollution abatement or control. Monitor effects of pollution and land degradation and recommend means of prevention or control. Design and direct studies to obtain technical environmental information about planned projects. Conduct applied research on topics such as waste control and treatment and pollution control methods.

— EYE OPENERS —

The strongest job growth should be in private-sector consulting firms.

- Annual earnings (average): $52,630
- Annual earnings (starting): $32,910
- Employed: 73,000
- Growth: 17.1%
- Annual job openings: 8,000

PREPARING FOR THE JOB

Education/training required: Master's degree.

Programs: Environmental science; environmental studies.

Knowledge/courses: Biology; geography; chemistry; law and government; engineering and technology; physics; design; public safety and security.

Licensure/certification: Certification available in some specializations.

WORKING CONDITIONS

Physical: More often indoors than outdoors; noisy; sitting.

Work settings: Partly in the field, partly in offices and laboratories.

Other job characteristics: Need to be exact or accurate; repeat same tasks.

OTHER FACTS

O*NET code: 19-2041.00

GOE information: Interest area: 15. Scientific Research, Engineering, and Mathematics. Work group: 15.03. Life Sciences.

Personality type: Investigative. Investigative occupations frequently involve working with ideas and require an extensive amount of thinking. These occupations can involve searching for facts and figuring out problems.

TOP SKILLS

- Science
- Service orientation
- Negotiation
- Coordination
- Reading comprehension
- Complex problem solving

WHERE TO FIND OUT MORE

Information on training and career opportunities for environmental scientists is available from

➤ American Geological Institute, 4220 King St., Alexandria, VA 22302-1502. Internet: www.agiweb.org

For career information and a list of education and training programs in oceanography and related fields, contact

➤ Marine Technology Society, 5565 Sterrett Place, Suite 108, Columbia, MD 21004. Internet: www.mtsociety.org

Epidemiologists

QUICK LOOK

Investigate and describe the determinants and distribution of disease, disability, and other health outcomes and develop the means for prevention and control. Oversee public health programs, including statistical analysis, health-care planning, surveillance systems, and public health improvement. Investigate diseases or parasites to determine cause and risk factors, progress, life cycle, or mode of transmission. Plan and direct studies to investigate human or animal disease, preventive methods, and treatments for disease. Plan, administer, and evaluate health safety standards and programs to improve public health, conferring with health department, industry personnel, physicians, and others. Provide expertise in the design, management, and evaluation of study protocols and health status questionnaires, sample selection, and analysis. Conduct research to develop methodologies, instrumentation, and procedures for medical application, analyzing data and presenting findings. Consult with and advise physicians, educators, researchers, government health officials, and others regarding medical applications of sciences such as physics, biology, and chemistry. Supervise professional, technical, and clerical personnel. Identify and analyze public health issues related to foodborne parasitic diseases and their impact on public policies or scientific studies or surveys. Teach principles of medicine and medical and laboratory procedures to physicians, residents, students, and technicians. Standardize drug dosages, methods of immunization, and procedures for manufacture of drugs and medicinal compounds. Prepare and analyze samples to study effects of drugs, gases, pesticides, or microorganisms on cell structure and tissue.

— EYE OPENERS —

Despite projected rapid job growth, competition is expected for most positions.

- Annual earnings (average): $52,170
- Annual earnings (starting): $33,620
- Employed: 5,000
- Growth: 26.2%
- Annual job openings: 1,000

PREPARING FOR THE JOB

Education/training required: Master's degree.

Programs: Biophysics; cell/cellular biology and histology; epidemiology; medical scientist (MS, PhD).

Knowledge/courses: Biology; sociology and anthropology; medicine and dentistry; English language; mathematics; computers and electronics; education and training; psychology.

Licensure/certification: Licensure required for those working as medical doctors; certification available.

WORKING CONDITIONS

Physical: Indoors; noisy; sitting; repetitive motions.

Work settings: Offices or laboratories.

Other job characteristics: Need to be exact or accurate; repeat same tasks.

OTHER FACTS

O*NET code: 19-1041.00

GOE information: Interest area: 15. Scientific Research, Engineering, and Mathematics. Work group: 15.03. Life Sciences.

```
—— TOP SKILLS ——
• Science
• Programming
• Reading comprehension
• Mathematics
• Writing
• Complex problem solving
```

Personality type: Investigative. Investigative occupations frequently involve working with ideas and require an extensive amount of thinking. These occupations can involve searching for facts and figuring out problems.

WHERE TO FIND OUT MORE

For more information about this career, contact

➤ American Society for Microbiology, Education Department, 1752 N St. NW, Washington, DC 20036-2804. Internet: www.asm.org

➤ World Health Organization. Internet: www.who.int/topics/epidemiology/en/

➤ American College of Epidemiology, 1500 Sunday Dr., Suite 102, Raleigh, NC 27607. Internet: www.acepidemiology2.org/

video number **55**

Mental Health Counselors

QUICK LOOK

Counsel with emphasis on prevention. Work with individuals and groups to promote opti-mum mental health. **May help individuals deal with addictions and substance abuse; fam-ily, parenting, and marital problems; suicide; stress management; problems with self-esteem; and issues associated with aging and mental and emotional health.** Maintain confidentiality of records relating to clients' treatment. Guide clients in the development of skills and strategies for dealing with their problems. Encourage clients to express their feel-ings and discuss what is happening in their lives and help them to develop insight into them-selves and their relationships. Prepare and maintain all required treatment records and reports. Counsel clients and patients, individually and in group sessions, to assist in overcom-ing dependencies, adjusting to life, and making changes. Collect information about clients through interviews, observation, and tests. Act as client advocates to coordinate required ser-vices or to resolve emergency problems in cri-sis situations. Develop and implement treatment plans based on clinical experience and knowledge. Collaborate with other staff members to perform clinical assessments and develop treatment plans. Evaluate clients' physical or mental condition based on review of client information. Meet with families, pro-bation officers, police, and other interested parties to exchange necessary information dur-ing the treatment process. Refer patients, clients, or family members to community resources or to specialists as necessary. Evaluate the effectiveness of counseling programs and clients' progress in resolving identified problems and moving towards defined objectives. Counsel family members to assist them in understanding, dealing with, and supporting clients or patients. Plan, organize, and lead structured programs of counseling, work, study, recreation, and social activities for clients. Modify treatment activities and approaches as needed to comply with changes in clients' status. Learn about new developments in the field by reading professional literature, attending courses and seminars, and establishing and main-taining contact with other social service agencies. Discuss with individual patients their plans for life after leaving therapy. Gather information about community mental health needs and resources that could be used in conjunction with therapy. Monitor clients' use of medications. Supervise other counselors, social service staff, and assistants.

— EYE OPENERS —

To be licensed, you must earn a master's degree in counseling or a closely related mental health discipline, complete a mini-mum of two years of additional supervised clinical work, and pass a state-developed or national licensure or certification examina-tion.

- Annual earnings (average): $34,010
- Annual earnings (starting): $21,760
- Employed: 96,000
- Growth: 27.2%
- Annual job openings: 14,000

© JIST Works

PREPARING FOR THE JOB

Education/training required: Master's degree.

Programs: Clinical/medical social work; mental and social health services and allied professions; mental health counseling/counselor training; substance abuse/addiction counseling.

Knowledge/courses: Therapy and counseling; psychology; sociology and anthropology; philosophy and theology; medicine and dentistry; education and training; customer and personal service; law and government.

Licensure/certification: Licensure required; certification available.

WORKING CONDITIONS

Physical: Indoors; noisy; sitting.

Work settings: Offices, perhaps located in a community agency.

Other job characteristics: None significant.

OTHER FACTS

O*NET code: 21-1014.00

GOE information: Interest area: 10. Human Service. Work group: 10.01. Counseling and Social Work.

TOP SKILLS

- Social perceptiveness
- Service orientation
- Negotiation
- Persuasion
- Learning strategies
- Active listening

Personality type: Social. Social occupations frequently involve working with, communicating with, and teaching people. These occupations often involve helping or providing service to others.

WHERE TO FIND OUT MORE

For general information about counseling, as well as information on specialties such as college, mental health, rehabilitation, multicultural, career, marriage and family, and gerontological counseling, contact

➤ American Counseling Association, 5999 Stevenson Ave., Alexandria, VA 22304-3300. Internet: www.counseling.org

For information on accredited counseling and related training programs, contact

➤ Council for Accreditation of Counseling and Related Educational Programs, 1001 N. Fairfax St., Suite 510, Alexandria, VA 22314. Internet: www.cacrep.org

Occupational Health and Safety Specialists

QUICK LOOK

Review, evaluate, and analyze work environments and design programs and procedures to control, eliminate, and prevent disease or injury caused by chemical, physical, and biological agents or ergonomic factors. May conduct inspections and enforce adherence to laws and regulations governing the health and safety of individuals. May be employed in the public or private sector. Order suspension of activities that pose threats to workers' health and safety. Recommend measures to help protect workers from potentially hazardous work methods, processes, or materials. Investigate accidents to identify causes and to determine how such accidents might be prevented in the future. Investigate the adequacy of ventilation, exhaust equipment, lighting, and other conditions that could affect employee health, comfort, or performance. Develop and maintain hygiene programs such as noise surveys, continuous atmosphere monitoring, ventilation surveys, and asbestos management plans. Inspect and evaluate workplace environments, equipment, and practices to ensure compliance with safety standards and government regulations. Collaborate with engineers and physicians to institute control and remedial measures for hazardous and potentially hazardous conditions or equipment. Conduct safety training and education programs and demonstrate the use of safety equipment. Provide new-employee health and safety orientations and develop materials for these presentations. Collect samples of dust, gases, vapors, and other potentially toxic materials for analysis. Investigate health-related complaints and inspect facilities to ensure that they comply with public health legislation and regulations. Coordinate "right-to-know" programs regarding hazardous chemicals and other substances. Maintain and update emergency response plans and procedures. Develop and maintain medical monitoring programs for employees. Conduct audits at hazardous waste sites or industrial sites and participate in hazardous waste site investigations. Inspect specified areas to ensure the presence of fire prevention equipment, safety equipment, and first-aid supplies. Collect samples of hazardous materials or arrange for sample collection. Maintain inventories of hazardous materials and hazardous wastes, using waste tracking systems to ensure that materials are handled properly. Prepare hazardous, radioactive, and mixed waste samples for transportation and storage by treating, compacting, packaging, and labeling them.

— EYE OPENERS —

About two out of five specialists worked in federal, state, and local government agencies that enforce rules on safety, health, and the environment.

- Annual earnings (average): $53,710
- Annual earnings (starting): $32,500
- Employed: 40,000
- Growth: 12.4%
- Annual job openings: 3,000

PREPARING FOR THE JOB

Education/training required: Master's degree.

Programs: Environmental health; industrial safety technology/technician training; occupational health and industrial hygiene; occupational safety and health technology/technician training; quality control and safety technologies/technician training.

Knowledge/courses: Chemistry; biology; physics; engineering and technology; public safety and security; education and training; psychology; building and construction.

Licensure/certification: Certification available.

WORKING CONDITIONS

Physical: More often indoors than outdoors; noisy; contaminants; sitting.

Work settings: Offices and field locations where working conditions are studied.

Other job characteristics: Need to be exact or accurate; errors have important consequences.

TOP SKILLS

- Science
- Management of financial resources
- Technology design
- Persuasion
- Systems analysis
- Management of material resources

OTHER FACTS

O*NET code: 29-9011.00

GOE information: Interest area: 07. Government and Public Administration. Work group: 07.03. Regulations Enforcement.

Personality type: Social. Social occupations frequently involve working with, communicating with, and teaching people. These occupations often involve helping or providing service to others.

WHERE TO FIND OUT MORE

For information about this career, contact

➤ American Industrial Hygiene Association, 2700 Prosperity Ave., Suite 250, Fairfax, VA 22031. Internet: www.aiha.org

➤ American Board of Industrial Hygiene, 6015 W. St. Joseph, Suite 102, Lansing, MI 48917. Internet: www.abih.org

➤ American Society of Safety Engineers, 1800 E. Oakton St., Des Plaines, IL 60018. Internet: www.asse.org

Occupational Therapists

QUICK LOOK

Assess, plan, organize, and participate in rehabilitative programs that help restore vocational, homemaking, and daily living skills, as well as general independence, to people with disabilities. Complete and maintain necessary records. Evaluate patients' progress and prepare reports that detail progress. Test and evaluate patients' physical and mental abilities and analyze medical data to determine realistic rehabilitation goals for patients. Select activities that will help individuals learn work and life-management skills within limits of their mental and physical capabilities. Plan, organize, and conduct occupational therapy programs in hospital, institutional, or community settings to help rehabilitate those impaired because of illness, injury, or psychological or developmental problems. Recommend changes in patients' work or living environments consistent with their needs and capabilities. Consult with rehabilitation team to select activity programs and coordinate occupational therapy with other therapeutic activities. Help clients improve decision-making, abstract reasoning, memory, sequencing, coordination, and perceptual skills by using computer programs. Develop and participate in health promotion programs, group activities, or discussions to promote client health, facilitate social adjustment, alleviate stress, and prevent physical or mental disability. Provide training and supervision in therapy techniques and objectives for students and nurses and other medical staff. Design and create, or requisition, special supplies and equipment, such as splints, braces, and computer-aided adaptive equipment. Plan and implement programs and social activities to help patients learn work and school skills and adjust to handicaps. Lay out materials such as puzzles, scissors, and eating utensils for use in therapy; clean and repair these tools after therapy sessions. Advise on health risks in the workplace and on health-related transition to retirement. Conduct research in occupational therapy. Provide patients with assistance in locating and holding jobs.

EYE OPENERS

More than a quarter of occupational therapists work part-time.

- Annual earnings (average): $56,860
- Annual earnings (starting): $38,840
- Employed: 92,000
- Growth: 33.6%
- Annual job openings: 7,000

PREPARING FOR THE JOB

Education/training required: Master's degree.

Programs: Occupational therapy/therapist training.

Knowledge/courses: Therapy and counseling; psychology; medicine and dentistry; customer and personal service; biology; sociology and anthropology; education and training; sales and marketing.

Licensure/certification: Licensure required.

WORKING CONDITIONS

Physical: Indoors; disease or infections; standing.

Work settings: Usually offices in hospitals and other health-care and community settings, but sometimes homes of clients or offices of service providers.

Other job characteristics: Need to be exact or accurate.

OTHER FACTS

O*NET code: 29-1122.00

GOE information: Interest area: 08. Health Science. Work group: 08.07. Medical Therapy.

— **TOP SKILLS** —

- Social perceptiveness
- Service orientation
- Science
- Technology design
- Reading comprehension
- Coordination

Personality type: Social. Social occupations frequently involve working with, communicating with, and teaching people. These occupations often involve helping or providing service to others.

WHERE TO FIND OUT MORE

For more information on occupational therapy as a career, contact

➤ American Occupational Therapy Association, 4720 Montgomery Ln., P.O. Box 31220, Bethesda, MD 20824-1220. Internet: www.aota.org

For information regarding the requirements to practice as an occupational therapist in schools, contact the appropriate occupational therapy regulatory agency for your state.

Physical Therapists

QUICK LOOK

Assess, plan, organize, and participate in rehabilitative programs that improve mobility, relieve pain, increase strength, and decrease or prevent deformity of patients suffering from disease or injury. Plan, prepare, and carry out individually designed programs of physical treatment to maintain, improve, or restore physical functioning; alleviate pain; and prevent physical dysfunction in patients. Perform and document an initial exam, evaluating data to identify problems and determine a diagnosis prior to intervention. Evaluate effects of treatment at various stages and adjust treatments to achieve maximum benefit. Administer manual exercises, massage, or traction to help relieve pain, increase patient strength, or decrease or prevent deformity or crippling. Instruct patient and family in treatment procedures to be continued at home. Confer with the patient, medical practitioners, and appropriate others to plan, implement, and assess the intervention program. Review the physician's referral and the patient's medical records to help determine the diagnosis and what physical therapy treatment is required. Obtain patients' informed consent to proposed interventions. Record prognosis, treatment, response, and progress in the patient's chart or enter information into a computer. Discharge patients from physical therapy when goals or projected outcomes have been attained and provide for appropriate follow-up care or referrals. Test and measure a patient's strength, motor development and function; sensory perception; functional capacity; and respiratory and circulatory efficiency and record data. Identify and document goals, anticipated progress, and plans for reevaluation. Provide information to the patient about the proposed intervention, its material risks and expected benefits, and any reasonable alternatives. Inform patients when the diagnosis reveals findings outside physical therapy and refer them to appropriate practitioners. Direct, supervise, assess, and communicate with supportive personnel. Administer treatment involving application of physical agents, using equipment, moist packs, ultraviolet and infrared lamps, and ultrasound machines. Teach physical therapy students as well as those in other health professions. Evaluate, fit, and adjust prosthetic and orthotic devices and recommend modification to orthotist. Provide educational information about physical therapy and physical therapists, injury prevention, ergonomics, and ways to promote health.

EYE OPENERS

Physical therapists are expected to continue professional development by participating in continuing education courses and workshops.

- Annual earnings (average): $63,080
- Annual earnings (starting): $44,750
- Employed: 155,000
- Growth: 36.7%
- Annual job openings: 13,000

PREPARING FOR THE JOB

Education/training required: Master's degree.

Programs: Kinesiotherapy/kinesiotherapist training; physical therapy/therapist training.

Knowledge/courses: Therapy and counseling; medicine and dentistry; psychology; biology; sociology and anthropology; customer and personal service; education and training; physics.

Licensure/certification: Licensure required.

WORKING CONDITIONS

Physical: Indoors; contaminants; disease or infections; standing; walking and running; bending or twisting the body.

Work settings: Hospitals, clinics, and private offices that have specially equipped facilities; or patients' hospital rooms, homes, or schools.

Other job characteristics: Need to be exact or accurate; errors have important consequences.

TOP SKILLS

- Science
- Reading comprehension
- Social perceptiveness
- Instructing
- Learning strategies
- Service orientation

OTHER FACTS

O*NET code: 29-1123.00

GOE information: Interest area: 08. Health Science. Work group: 08.07. Medical Therapy.

Personality type: Social. Social occupations frequently involve working with, communicating with, and teaching people. These occupations often involve helping or providing service to others.

WHERE TO FIND OUT MORE

Additional career information and a list of accredited educational programs in physical therapy are available from

➤ American Physical Therapy Association, 1111 N. Fairfax St., Alexandria, VA 22314-1488. Internet: www.apta.org

Rehabilitation Counselors

QUICK LOOK

Counsel individuals to maximize the independence and employability of persons coping with personal, social, and vocational difficulties that result from birth defects, illness, disease, accidents, or the stress of daily life. Coordinate activities for residents of care and treatment facilities. Assess client needs and design and implement rehabilitation programs that may include personal and vocational counseling, training, and job placement. Monitor and record clients' progress in order to ensure that goals and objectives are met. Confer with clients to discuss their options and goals in order to develop rehabilitation programs and plans for accessing needed services. Prepare and maintain records and case files, including documentation such as clients' personal and eligibility information, services provided, narratives of client contacts, and relevant correspondence. Arrange for physical, mental, academic, vocational, and other evaluations to obtain information for assessing clients' needs and developing rehabilitation plans. Analyze information from interviews, educational and medical records, consultation with other professionals, and diagnostic evaluations to assess clients' abilities, needs, and eligibility for services. Develop rehabilitation plans that fit clients' aptitudes, education levels, physical abilities, and career goals. Maintain close contact with clients during job training and placements to resolve problems and evaluate

EYE OPENERS

Graduate programs in this field typically require two years of full-time study and field work, but they usually allow students to attend on a part-time basis.

- Annual earnings (average): $28,330
- Annual earnings (starting): $18,750
- Employed: 131,000
- Growth: 23.9%
- Annual job openings: 19,000

placement adequacy. Identify barriers to client employment, such as inaccessible work sites, inflexible schedules, and transportation problems, and work with clients to develop strategies for overcoming these barriers. Develop and maintain relationships with community referral sources, such as schools and community groups. Arrange for on-site job coaching or assistive devices, such as specially equipped wheelchairs, in order to help clients adapt to work or school environments. Confer with physicians, psychologists, occupational therapists, and other professionals to develop and implement client rehabilitation programs. Develop diagnostic procedures for determining clients' needs. Participate in job development and placement programs, contacting prospective employers, placing clients in jobs, and evaluating the success of placements. Collaborate with clients' families to implement rehabilitation plans that include behavioral, residential, social, and/or employment goals. Collaborate with community agencies to establish facilities and programs to assist persons with disabilities.

PREPARING FOR THE JOB

Education/training required: Master's degree.

Programs: Assistive/augmentative technology and rehabiliation engineering; vocational rehabilitation counseling/counselor training.

Knowledge/courses: Psychology; therapy and counseling; philosophy and theology; education and training; personnel and human resources; sales and marketing; sociology and anthropology; medicine and dentistry.

Licensure/certification: Licensure required; certification available.

WORKING CONDITIONS

Physical: More often indoors than outdoors; sitting; walking and running.

Work settings: Offices, perhaps located in a community agency.

Other job characteristics: Need to be exact or accurate; repeat same tasks.

OTHER FACTS

O*NET code: 21-1015.00

GOE information: Interest area: 10. Human Service. Work group: 10.01. Counseling and Social Work.

Personality type: No data available.

TOP SKILLS

- Management of financial resources
- Social perceptiveness
- Writing
- Service orientation
- Monitoring
- Coordination

WHERE TO FIND OUT MORE

For general information about counseling, as well as information on specialties such as college, mental health, rehabilitation, multicultural, career, marriage and family, and gerontological counseling, contact

➤ American Counseling Association, 5999 Stevenson Ave., Alexandria, VA 22304-3300. Internet: www.counseling.org

For information on accredited counseling and related training programs, contact

➤ Council for Accreditation of Counseling and Related Educational Programs, 1001 N. Fairfax St., Suite 510, Alexandria, VA 22314. Internet: www.cacrep.org

Speech-Language Pathologists

QUICK LOOK

Assess and treat persons with speech, language, voice, and fluency disorders. May select alternative communication systems and teach their use. May perform research related to speech and language problems. Monitor patients' progress and adjust treatments accordingly. Evaluate hearing and speech/language test results and medical or background information to diagnose and plan treatment for speech, language, fluency, voice, and swallowing disorders. Administer hearing or speech and language evaluations, tests, or examinations to patients in order to collect information on the type and degree of impairments, using written and oral tests and special instruments. Record information on the initial evaluation, treatment, progress, and discharge of clients. Develop and implement treatment plans for problems such as stuttering, delayed language, swallowing disorders, and inappropriate pitch or harsh voice problems, based on own assessments and recommendations of physicians, psychologists, or social workers. Develop individual or group programs in schools to deal with speech or language problems. Instruct clients in techniques for more effective communication, including sign language, lip reading, and voice improvement. Teach clients to control or strengthen tongue, jaw, face muscles, and breathing mechanisms. Develop speech exercise programs to reduce disabilities. Consult with and advise educators or medical staff on speech or hearing topics, such as communication strategies or speech and language stimulation. Instruct patients and family members in strategies to cope with or avoid communication-related misunderstandings. Design, develop, and employ alternative diagnostic or communication devices and strategies. Conduct lessons and direct educational or therapeutic games to assist teachers dealing with students' speech problems. Refer clients to additional medical or educational services if needed. Participate in conferences or training, or publish research results, in order to share knowledge of new hearing or speech disorder treatment methods or technologies. Communicate with nonspeaking students, using sign language or computer technology. Provide communication instruction to dialect speakers or students with limited English proficiency. Use computer applications to identify and assist with communication disabilities.

EYE OPENERS

About half of all speech-language pathologists work in educational services, and most others are employed by health care and social assistance facilities.

- Annual earnings (average): $54,880
- Annual earnings (starting): $36,380
- Employed: 96,000
- Growth: 14.6%
- Annual job openings: 5,000

PREPARING FOR THE JOB

Education/training required: Master's degree.

Programs: Audiology/audiologist and speech-language pathology/pathologist training; communication disorders sciences and services; communication disorders; speech-language pathology/pathologist training.

Knowledge/courses: Therapy and counseling; psychology; education and training; sociology and anthropology; medicine and dentistry; English language; philosophy and theology; communications and media.

Licensure/certification: Licensure required in almost all states; certification available.

WORKING CONDITIONS

Physical: Indoors; disease or infections; sitting.

Work settings: Hospitals and other health-care facilities, schools, and patients' homes.

Other job characteristics: Need to be exact or accurate.

----- **TOP SKILLS** -----

- Instructing
- Learning strategies
- Social perceptiveness
- Speaking
- Monitoring
- Service orientation

OTHER FACTS

O*NET code: 29-1127.00

GOE information: Interest area: 08. Health Science. Work group: 08.07. Medical Therapy.

Personality type: Social. Social occupations frequently involve working with, communicating with, and teaching people. These occupations often involve helping or providing service to others.

WHERE TO FIND OUT MORE

State licensing boards can provide information on licensure requirements. State departments of education can supply information on certification requirements for those who want to work in public schools.

For information on careers in speech-language pathology, a description of the CCC-SLP credential, and a listing of accredited graduate programs in speech-language pathology, contact

➤ American Speech-Language-Hearing Association, 10801 Rockville Pike, Rockville, MD 20852. Internet: www.asha.org

Clinical Psychologists

QUICK LOOK

Diagnose or evaluate mental and emotional disorders of individuals through observation, interview, and psychological tests and formulate and administer treatment programs. Identify psychological, emotional, or behavioral issues and diagnose disorders, using information obtained from interviews, tests, records, and reference materials. Develop and implement individual treatment plans, specifying type, frequency, intensity, and duration of therapy. Interact with clients to assist them in gaining insight, defining goals, and planning action to achieve effective personal, social, educational, and vocational development and adjustment. Discuss the treatment of problems with clients. Utilize a variety of treatment methods such as psychotherapy, hypnosis, behavior modification, stress reduction therapy, psychodrama, and play therapy. Counsel individuals and groups regarding problems such as stress, substance abuse, and family situations to modify behavior or to improve personal, social, and vocational adjustment. Write reports on clients and maintain required paperwork. Evaluate the effectiveness of counseling or treatments and the accuracy and completeness of diagnoses; then modify plans and diagnoses as necessary. Obtain and study medical, psychological, social, and family histories by interviewing individuals, couples, or families and by reviewing records. Consult reference material such as textbooks, manuals, and journals to identify symptoms, make diagnoses, and develop approaches to treatment. Maintain current knowledge of relevant research. Observe individuals at play, in group interactions, or in other contexts to detect indications of mental deficiency, abnormal behavior, or maladjustment. Select, administer, score, and interpret psychological tests to obtain information on individuals' intelligence, achievements, interests, and personalities. Refer clients to other specialists, institutions, or support services as necessary. Develop, direct, and participate in training programs for staff and students. Provide psychological or administrative services and advice to private firms and community agencies regarding mental health programs or individual cases. Provide occupational, educational, and other information to individuals so that they can make educational and vocational plans.

— EYE OPENERS —

About 4 out of 10 psychologists are self-employed, compared with less than 1 out of 10 among all professional workers.

- Annual earnings (average): $57,170
- Annual earnings (starting): $34,040
- Employed: 167,000
- Growth: 19.1%
- Annual job openings: 10,000

Our sources did not provide separate job openings data for this occupation. The figures for employment and job openings listed here are shared with counseling psychologists and with school psychologists.

PREPARING FOR THE JOB

Education/training required: Doctoral degree.

Programs: Clinical child psychology; clinical psychology; counseling psychology; developmental and child psychology; psychoanalysis and psychotherapy; psychology; school psychology.

Knowledge/courses: Therapy and counseling; psychology; sociology and anthropology; philosophy and theology; customer and personal service; medicine and dentistry; education and training; English language.

Licensure/certification: Licensure required.

WORKING CONDITIONS

Physical: Indoors; sitting.

Work settings: Offices, perhaps located in a hospital, nursing home, or other health-care facility.

Other job characteristics: Need to be exact or accurate.

TOP SKILLS

- Social perceptiveness
- Service orientation
- Complex problem solving
- Learning strategies
- Negotiation
- Active listening

OTHER FACTS

O*NET code: 19-3031.02

GOE information: Interest area: 10. Human Service. Work group: 10.01. Counseling and Social Work.

Personality type: Investigative. Investigative occupations frequently involve working with ideas and require an extensive amount of thinking. These occupations can involve searching for facts and figuring out problems.

WHERE TO FIND OUT MORE

For information on careers, educational requirements, financial assistance, and licensing in all fields of psychology, contact

➤ American Psychological Association, Education Directorate, 750 First St. NE, Washington, DC 20002-4242. Internet: www.apa.org/students

For information on careers, educational requirements, certification, and licensing of school psychologists, contact

➤ National Association of School Psychologists, 4340 East West Hwy., Suite 402, Bethesda, MD 20814. Internet: www.nasponline.org

Counseling Psychologists

QUICK LOOK

Assess and evaluate individuals' problems through the use of case history, interview, and observation and provide individual or group counseling services to assist individuals in achieving more effective personal, social, educational, and vocational development and adjustment. Collect information about individuals by using interviews, case histories, observational techniques, and other assessment methods. Counsel individuals, groups, or families to help them understand problems, define goals, and develop realistic action plans. Develop therapeutic and treatment plans based on clients' interests, abilities, and needs. Consult with other professionals to discuss therapies, treatments, counseling resources, or techniques and to share occupational information. Analyze data such as interview notes, test results, and reference manuals in order to identify symptoms and to diagnose the nature of clients' problems. Advise clients on how they could be helped by counseling. Evaluate the results of counseling methods to determine the reliability and validity of treatments. Provide consulting services to schools, social service agencies, and businesses. Refer clients to specialists or to other institutions for noncounseling treatment of problems. Select, administer, and interpret psychological tests to assess intelligence, aptitudes, abilities, or interests. Conduct research to develop or improve diagnostic or therapeutic counseling techniques.

EYE OPENERS

Competition for admission to graduate psychology programs is keen.

- Annual earnings (average): $57,170
- Annual earnings (starting): $34,040
- Employed: 167,000
- Growth: 19.1%
- Annual job openings: 10,000

Our sources did not provide separate job openings data for this occupation. The figures for employment and job openings listed here are shared with clinical psychologists and with school psychologists.

PREPARING FOR THE JOB

Education/training required: Doctoral degree.

Programs: Clinical child psychology; clinical psychology; counseling psychology; developmental and child psychology; psychoanalysis and psychotherapy; psychology, general; school psychology.

Knowledge/courses: Therapy and counseling; philosophy and theology; sociology and anthropology; psychology; English language; customer and personal service; education and training; law and government.

Licensure/certification: Licensure required.

WORKING CONDITIONS

Physical: Indoors; sitting.

Work settings: Offices, perhaps located in a hospital, nursing home, or other health-care facility.

Other job characteristics: Need to be exact or accurate.

TOP SKILLS

- Social perceptiveness
- Active listening
- Persuasion
- Service orientation
- Negotiation
- Coordination

OTHER FACTS

O*NET code: 19-3031.03

GOE information: Interest area: 10. Human Service. Work group: 10.01. Counseling and Social Work.

Personality type: Social. Social occupations frequently involve working with, communicating with, and teaching people. These occupations often involve helping or providing service to others.

WHERE TO FIND OUT MORE

For information on careers, educational requirements, financial assistance, and licensing in all fields of psychology, contact

➤ American Psychological Association, Education Directorate, 750 First St. NE, Washington, DC 20002-4242. Internet: www.apa.org/students

For information on careers, educational requirements, certification, and licensing of school psychologists, contact

➤ National Association of School Psychologists, 4340 East West Hwy., Suite 402, Bethesda, MD 20814. Internet: www.nasponline.org

QUICK LOOK

Adjust spinal column and other articulations of the body to correct abnormalities of the human body believed to be caused by interference with the nervous system. Examine patient to determine nature and extent of disorder. Manipulate spine or other involved area. May utilize supplementary measures, such as exercise, rest, water, light, heat, and nutritional therapy. Perform a series of manual adjustments to the spine, or other articulations of the body, to correct the musculoskeletal system. Evaluate the functioning of the neuromuscularskeletal system and the spine, using systems of chiropractic diagnosis. Diagnose health problems by reviewing patients' health and medical histories; questioning, observing, and examining patients; and interpreting X-rays. Maintain accurate case histories of patients.

Advise patients about recommended courses of treatment. Obtain and record patients' medical histories. Analyze X-rays to locate the sources of patients' difficulties and to rule out fractures or diseases as sources of problems. Counsel patients about nutrition, exercise, sleeping habits, stress management, and other matters. Arrange for diagnostic X-rays to be taken. Consult with and refer patients to appropriate health practitioners when necessary. Suggest and apply the use of supports such as straps, tapes, bandages, and braces if necessary.

EYE OPENERS

Chiropractors must be licensed, which requires two to four years of undergraduate education, the completion of a four-year chiropractic college course, and passing scores on national and state examinations.

- Annual earnings (average): $67,200
- Annual earnings (starting): $32,900
- Employed: 53,000
- Growth: 22.4%
- Annual job openings: 4,000

PREPARING FOR THE JOB

Education/training required: First professional degree.

Programs: Chiropractic (DC).

Knowledge/courses: Medicine and dentistry; therapy and counseling; biology; psychology; sales and marketing; customer and personal service; personnel and human resources; clerical practices.

Licensure/certification: Licensure required.

WORKING CONDITIONS

Physical: Indoors; disease or infections; standing; using hands on objects, tools, or controls; bending or twisting the body; repetitive motions.

Work settings: Offices.

Other job characteristics: Need to be exact or accurate; repeat same tasks; errors have important consequences.

OTHER FACTS

O*NET code: 29-1011.00

GOE information: Interest area: 08. Health Science. Work group: 08.04. Health Specialties.

TOP SKILLS

- Science
- Social perceptiveness
- Management of financial resources
- Persuasion
- Service orientation
- Reading comprehension

Personality type: Investigative. Investigative occupations frequently involve working with ideas and require an extensive amount of thinking. These occupations can involve searching for facts and figuring out problems.

WHERE TO FIND OUT MORE

General information on a career as a chiropractor is available from the following organizations:

➤ American Chiropractic Association, 1701 Clarendon Blvd., Arlington, VA 22209. Internet: www.acatoday.org

➤ International Chiropractors Association, 1110 N. Glebe Rd., Suite 650, Arlington, VA 22201. Internet: www.chiropractic.org

➤ World Chiropractic Alliance, 2950 N. Dobson Rd., Suite 3, Chandler, AZ 85224. Internet: www.worldchiropracticalliance.org

First Professional Degree

Quick Look

Diagnose and treat diseases, injuries, and malformations of teeth and gums and related oral structures. May treat diseases of nerve, pulp, and other dental tissues affecting vitality of teeth. Use masks, gloves, and safety glasses to protect themselves and their patients from infectious diseases. Administer anesthetics to limit the amount of pain experienced by patients during procedures. Examine teeth, gums, and related tissues, using dental instruments, X-rays, and other diagnostic equipment, in order to evaluate dental health, diagnose diseases or abnormalities, and plan appropriate treatments. Formulate plan of treatment for patient's teeth and mouth tissue. Use air turbine and hand instruments, dental appliances, and surgical implements. Advise and instruct patients regarding preventive dental care, the causes and treatment of dental problems, and oral health-care services. Design, make, and fit prosthodontic appliances, such as space maintainers, bridges, and dentures, or write fabrication instructions or prescriptions for denturists and dental technicians. Provide preventive and corrective services for teeth, gums, and related oral structures. Fill pulp chamber and canal with endodontic materials. Write prescriptions for antibiotics and other medications. Analyze and evaluate dental needs to determine changes and trends in patterns of dental disease. Treat exposure of pulp by pulp capping, removal of pulp from pulp chamber, or root canal, using dental instruments. Eliminate irritating margins of fillings and correct occlusions, using dental instruments. Perform oral and periodontal surgery on the jaw or mouth. Remove diseased tissue, using surgical instruments. Apply fluoride and sealants to teeth. Manage business, employing and supervising staff and handling paperwork and insurance claims. Bleach, clean, or polish teeth to restore natural color. Plan, organize, and maintain dental health programs. Produce and evaluate dental health educational materials.

EYE OPENERS

Most dentists are solo practitioners.

- Annual earnings (average): $125,300
- Annual earnings (starting): $64,770
- Employed: 128,000
- Growth: 13.5%
- Annual job openings: 7,000

PREPARING FOR THE JOB

Education/training required: First professional degree.

Programs: Advanced general dentistry (Cert, MS, PhD); dental clinical sciences (MS, PhD); dental materials (MS, PhD); dental public health and education (Cert, MS/MPH, PhD/DPH); dental public health specialty; dentistry (DDS, DMD); oral biology and oral pathology (MS, PhD); pediatric dentistry/pedodontics (Cert, MS, PhD); pedodontics specialty.

Knowledge/courses: Medicine and dentistry; biology; psychology; personnel and human resources; chemistry; economics and accounting; sales and marketing; engineering and technology.

Licensure/certification: Licensure required; licensure or certification sometimes required for certain specializations.

WORKING CONDITIONS

Physical: Indoors; contaminants; radiation; disease or infections; sitting; using hands on objects, tools, or controls.

Work settings: Offices.

Other job characteristics: Need to be exact or accurate; errors have important consequences; repeat same tasks.

─── TOP SKILLS ───

- Science
- Management of financial resources
- Management of material resources
- Complex problem solving
- Equipment selection
- Management of personnel resources

OTHER FACTS

O*NET code: 29-1021.00

GOE information: Interest area: 08. Health Science. Work group: 08.03. Dentistry.

Personality type: Investigative. Investigative occupations frequently involve working with ideas and require an extensive amount of thinking. These occupations can involve searching for facts and figuring out problems.

WHERE TO FIND OUT MORE

For information on dentistry as a career, a list of accredited dental schools, and a list of state boards of dental examiners, contact

➤ American Dental Association, Commission on Dental Accreditation, 211 E. Chicago Ave., Chicago, IL 60611-2678. Internet: www.ada.org

For information on admission to dental schools, contact

➤ American Dental Education Association, 1400 K St. NW, Suite 1100, Washington, DC 20005. Internet: www.adea.org

First Professional Degree

Family and General Practitioners

QUICK LOOK

Diagnose, treat, and help prevent diseases and injuries that commonly occur in the general population. Prescribe or administer treatment, therapy, medication, vaccination, and other specialized medical care to treat or prevent illness, disease, or injury. Order, perform, and interpret tests and analyze records, reports, and examination information to diagnose patients' condition. Monitor the patients' conditions and progress and reevaluate treatments as necessary. Explain procedures and discuss test results or prescribed treatments with patients. Collect, record, and maintain patient information, such as medical history, reports, and examination results. Advise patients and community members concerning diet, activity, hygiene, and disease prevention. Refer patients to medical specialists or other practitioners when necessary. Direct and coordinate activities of nurses, students, assistants, specialists, therapists, and other medical staff. Coordinate work with nurses, social workers, rehabilitation therapists, pharmacists, psychologists, and other health-care providers. Deliver babies. Operate on patients to remove, repair, or improve functioning of diseased or injured body parts and systems. Plan, implement, or administer health programs or standards in hospital, business, or community for information, prevention, or treatment of injury or illness. Prepare reports for government or management of birth, death, and disease statistics; workforce evaluations; or medical status of individuals. Conduct research to study anatomy and develop or test medications, treatments, or procedures to prevent or control disease or injury.

EYE OPENERS

Over one-third of full-time physicians work 60 or more hours a week.

- Annual earnings (average): $140,400
- Annual earnings (starting): $56,680
- Employed: 567,000
- Growth: 24.0%
- Annual job openings: 41,000

Our sources did not provide separate job openings data for this occupation. The figures for employment and job openings listed here are shared with anesthesiologists, internists, obstetricians and gynecologists, pediatricians, psychiatrists, and surgeons.

PREPARING FOR THE JOB

Education/training required: First professional degree.

Programs: Family medicine; medicine (MD); osteopathic medicine/osteopathy (DO).

Knowledge/courses: Medicine and dentistry; therapy and counseling; biology; psychology; sociology and anthropology; chemistry; customer and personal service; English language.

Licensure/certification: Licensure required; certification available for certain specializations.

WORKING CONDITIONS

Physical: Indoors; disease or infections; standing; using hands on objects, tools, or controls.

Work settings: Small private offices or clinics, group-practice offices or health-care organizations, or hospitals or other health-care facilities.

Other job characteristics: Need to be exact or accurate; errors have important consequences.

OTHER FACTS

O*NET code: 29-1062.00

GOE information: Interest area: 08. Health Science. Work group: 08.02. Medicine and Surgery.

Personality type: Investigative. Investigative occupations frequently involve working with ideas and require an extensive amount of thinking. These occupations can involve searching for facts and figuring out problems.

TOP SKILLS

- Science
- Social perceptiveness
- Reading comprehension
- Complex problem solving
- Persuasion
- Service orientation

WHERE TO FIND OUT MORE

For a list of medical schools and residency programs, as well as information on premedical education, financial aid, and medicine as a career, contact

➤ Association of American Medical Colleges, 2450 N St. NW, Washington, DC 20037-1126. Internet: www.aamc.org

➤ American Association of Colleges of Osteopathic Medicine, 5550 Friendship Blvd., Suite 310, Chevy Chase, MD 20815-7231. Internet: www.aacom.org

➤ American Medical Association, 515 N. State St., Chicago, IL 60610. Internet: www.ama-assn.org

➤ American Osteopathic Association, Division of Communications, 142 E. Ontario St., Chicago, IL 60611. Internet: www.osteopathic.org

First Professional Degree

Obstetricians and Gynecologists

QUICK LOOK

Diagnose, treat, and help prevent diseases of women, especially those affecting the reproductive system and the process of childbirth. Care for and treat women during prenatal, natal, and postnatal periods. Explain procedures and discuss test results or prescribed treatments with patients. Treat diseases of female organs. Monitor patients' condition and progress and reevaluate treatments as necessary. Perform cesarean sections or other surgical procedures as needed to preserve patients' health and deliver babies safely. Prescribe or administer therapy, medication, and other specialized medical care to treat or prevent illness, disease, or injury. Analyze records, reports, test results, or examination information to diagnose medical condition of patient. Collect, record, and maintain patient information, such as medical histories, reports, and examination results. Advise patients and community members concerning diet, activity, hygiene, and disease prevention. Refer patient to medical specialist or other practitioner when necessary. Consult with or provide consulting services to other physicians. Direct and coordinate activities of nurses, students, assistants, specialists, therapists, and other medical staff. Plan, implement, or administer health programs in hospitals, businesses, or communities for prevention and treatment of injuries or illnesses. Prepare government and organizational reports on birth, death, and disease statistics; workforce evaluations; or the medical status of individuals. Conduct research to develop or test medications, treatments, or procedures to prevent or control disease or injury.

— EYE OPENERS —

New physicians are much less likely to enter solo practice and more likely to work as salaried employees of group medical practices, clinics, hospitals, or health networks.

- Annual earnings (average): More than $145,600
- Annual earnings (starting): $95,960
- Employed: 567,000
- Growth: 24.0%
- Annual job openings: 41,000

Our sources did not provide separate job openings data for this occupation. The figures for employment and job openings listed here are shared with anesthesiologists, family and general practitioners, internists, pediatricians, psychiatrists, and surgeons.

PREPARING FOR THE JOB

Education/training required: First professional degree.

Programs: Neonatal-perinatal medicine; obstetrics and gynecology.

Knowledge/courses: Medicine and dentistry; therapy and counseling; biology; psychology; sociology and anthropology; chemistry; English language; philosophy and theology.

Licensure/certification: Licensure required; certification available for certain specializations.

WORKING CONDITIONS

Physical: Indoors; disease or infections; standing; using hands on objects, tools, or controls.

Work settings: Private offices or clinics, group-practice offices, health-care organizations, hospitals, and other health-care facilities.

Other job characteristics: Need to be exact or accurate; errors have important consequences.

OTHER FACTS

O*NET code: 29-1064.00

GOE information: Interest area: 08. Health Science. Work group: 08.02. Medicine and Surgery.

Personality type: Investigative. Investigative occupations frequently involve working with ideas and require an extensive amount of thinking. These occupations can involve searching for facts and figuring out problems.

--- TOP SKILLS ---

- Science
- Judgment and decision making
- Reading comprehension
- Active learning
- Complex problem solving
- Social perceptiveness

WHERE TO FIND OUT MORE

For information on medical education and medicine as a career, contact

➤ Association of American Medical Colleges, 2450 N St. NW, Washington, DC 20037-1126. Internet: www.aamc.org

➤ American Association of Colleges of Osteopathic Medicine, 5550 Friendship Blvd., Suite 310, Chevy Chase, MD 20815-7231. Internet: www.aacom.org

➤ American Medical Association, 515 N. State St., Chicago, IL 60610. Internet: www.ama-assn.org

➤ American College of Obstetricians and Gynecologists, 409 12th St. SW, P.O. Box 96920, Washington, DC 20090-6920. Internet: www.acog.org

First Professional Degree

Optometrists

QUICK LOOK

Diagnose, manage, and treat conditions and diseases of the human eye and visual system. Examine eyes and visual system, diagnose problems or impairments, prescribe corrective lenses, and provide treatment. May prescribe therapeutic drugs to treat specific eye conditions. Examine eyes, using observation, instruments, and pharmaceutical agents, in order to determine visual acuity and perception, focus, and coordination and to diagnose diseases and other abnormalities, such as glaucoma or color-blindness. Analyze test results and develop a treatment plan. Prescribe, supply, fit, and adjust eyeglasses, contact lenses, and other vision aids. Prescribe medications to treat eye diseases if state laws permit. Educate and counsel patients on contact lens care, visual hygiene, lighting arrangements, and safety factors. Consult with and refer patients to ophthalmologist or other health-care practitioner if additional medical treatment is determined necessary. Remove foreign bodies from the eye. Provide patients undergoing eye surgeries, such as cataract and laser vision correction, with pre-operative and postoperative care. Prescribe therapeutic procedures to correct or conserve vision. Provide vision therapy and low vision rehabilitation.

EYE OPENERS

To be licensed, optometrists must earn a doctor of optometry degree from an accredited optometry school and pass a written national board exam and a clinical examination.

- Annual earnings (average): $88,040
- Annual earnings (starting): $42,860
- Employed: 34,000
- Growth: 19.7%
- Annual job openings: 2,000

PREPARING FOR THE JOB

Education/training required: First professional degree.

Programs: Optometry (OD).

Knowledge/courses: Medicine and dentistry; biology; psychology; sales and marketing; economics and accounting; personnel and human resources; therapy and counseling; chemistry.

Licensure/certification: Licensure required.

WORKING CONDITIONS

Physical: Indoors; disease or infections; sitting; using hands on objects, tools, or controls; repetitive motions.

Work settings: Usually offices.

Other job characteristics: Need to be exact or accurate; errors have important consequences.

OTHER FACTS

O*NET code: 29-1041.00

GOE information: Interest area: 08. Health Science. Work group: 08.04. Health Specialties.

TOP SKILLS

- Science
- Judgment and decision making
- Management of personnel resources
- Active listening
- Reading comprehension
- Persuasion

Personality type: Investigative. Investigative occupations frequently involve working with ideas and require an extensive amount of thinking. These occupations can involve searching for facts and figuring out problems.

WHERE TO FIND OUT MORE

For information on optometry as a career and a list of accredited optometry schools, contact

➤ Association of Schools and Colleges of Optometry, 6110 Executive Blvd., Suite 510, Rockville, MD 20852. Internet: www.opted.org

Additional career information is available from

➤ American Optometric Association, Educational Services, 243 N. Lindbergh Blvd., St. Louis, MO 63141. Internet: www.aoanet.org

Pediatricians, General

QUICK LOOK

Diagnose, treat, and help prevent children's diseases and injuries. Examine patients or order, perform, and interpret diagnostic tests in order to obtain information on medical condition and determine diagnosis. Examine children regularly to assess their growth and development. Prescribe or administer treatment, therapy, medication, vaccination, and other specialized medical care to treat or prevent illness, disease, or injury in infants and children. Collect, record, and maintain patient information, such as medical history, reports, and examination results. Advise patients, parents or guardians, and community members concerning diet, activity, hygiene, and disease prevention. Treat children who have minor illnesses, acute and chronic health problems, and growth and development concerns. Explain procedures and discuss test results or prescribed treatments with patients and parents or guardians. Monitor patients' condition and progress and reevaluate treatments as necessary. Plan and execute medical care programs to aid in the mental and physical growth and development of children and adolescents. Refer patient to medical specialist or other practitioner when necessary. Direct and coordinate activities of nurses, students, assistants, specialists, therapists, and other medical staff. Provide consulting services to other physicians. Plan, implement, or administer health programs or standards in hospital, business, or community for information, prevention, or treatment of injury or illness. Operate on patients to remove, repair, or improve functioning of diseased or injured body parts and systems. Conduct research to study anatomy and develop or test medications, treatments, or procedures to prevent or control disease or injury. Prepare reports for government or management of birth, death, and disease statistics; workforce evaluations; or medical status of individuals.

── EYE OPENERS ──

Job opportunities should be very good, particularly in rural and low-income areas.

- Annual earnings (average): $136,600
- Annual earnings (starting): $66,520
- Employed: 567,000
- Growth: 24.0%
- Annual job openings: 41,000

Our sources did not provide separate job openings data for this occupation. The figures for employment and job openings listed here are shared with anesthesiologists, family and general practitioners, internists, obstetricians and gynecologists, psychiatrists, and surgeons.

Preparing for the Job

Education/training required: First professional degree.

Programs: Child/pediatric neurology; family medicine; neonatal-perinatal medicine; pediatric cardiology; pediatric endocrinology; pediatric hemato-oncology; pediatric nephrology; pediatric orthopedics; pediatric surgery; pediatrics.

Knowledge/courses: Medicine and dentistry; therapy and counseling; biology; psychology; chemistry; sociology and anthropology; personnel and human resources; English language.

Licensure/certification: Licensure required; certification available for certain specializations.

Working Conditions

Physical: Indoors; disease or infections; standing; using hands on objects, tools, or controls.

Work settings: Private offices or clinics, group-practice offices, health-care organizations, hospitals, and other health-care facilities.

Other job characteristics: Need to be exact or accurate; errors have important consequences.

```
─────── TOP SKILLS ───────

• Science
• Social perceptiveness
• Active learning
• Persuasion
• Critical thinking
• Management of financial resources
```

Other Facts

O*NET code: 29-1065.00

GOE information: Interest area: 08. Health Science. Work group: 08.02. Medicine and Surgery.

Personality type: Investigative. Investigative occupations frequently involve working with ideas and require an extensive amount of thinking. These occupations can involve searching for facts and figuring out problems.

Where to Find Out More

For a list of medical schools and residency programs, as well as information on premedical education, financial aid, and medicine as a career, contact

➤ Association of American Medical Colleges, 2450 N St. NW, Washington, DC 20037-1126. Internet: www.aamc.org

➤ American Association of Colleges of Osteopathic Medicine, 5550 Friendship Blvd., Suite 310, Chevy Chase, MD 20815-7231. Internet: www.aacom.org

➤ American Medical Association, 515 N. State St., Chicago, IL 60610. Internet: www.ama-assn.org

➤ American Academy of Pediatrics, 141 Northwest Point Blvd., Elk Grove Village, IL 60007-1098. Internet: www.aap.org

First Professional Degree

QUICK LOOK

Compound and dispense medications following prescriptions issued by physicians, dentists, or other authorized medical practitioners. Review prescriptions to assure accuracy, to ascertain the needed ingredients, and to evaluate their suitability. Provide information and advice regarding drug interactions, side effects, dosage, and proper medication storage. Analyze prescribing trends to monitor patient compliance and to prevent excessive usage or harmful interactions. Order and purchase pharmaceutical supplies, medical supplies, and drugs, maintaining stock and storing and handling it properly. Maintain records, such as pharmacy files; patient profiles; charge system files; inventories; control records for radioactive nuclei; and registries of poisons, narcotics, and controlled drugs. Provide specialized services to help patients manage conditions such as diabetes, asthma, smoking cessation, or high blood pressure. Advise customers on the selection of medication brands, medical equipment, and health-care supplies. Collaborate with other health-care professionals to plan, monitor, review, and evaluate the quality and effectiveness of drugs and drug regimens, providing advice on drug applications and characteristics. Compound and dispense medications as prescribed by doctors and dentists by calculating, weighing, measuring, and mixing ingredients or oversee these activities. Offer health promotion and prevention activities, for example, training people to use devices such as blood pressure or diabetes monitors. Refer patients to other health professionals and agencies when appropriate. Prepare sterile solutions and infusions for use in surgical procedures, emergency rooms, or patients' homes. Plan, implement, and maintain procedures for mixing, packaging, and labeling pharmaceuticals according to policy and legal requirements to ensure quality, security, and proper disposal. Assay radiopharmaceuticals, verify rates of disintegration, and calculate the volume required to produce the desired results to ensure proper dosages. Manage pharmacy operations by hiring and supervising staff, performing administrative duties, and buying and selling nonpharmaceutical merchandise. Work in hospitals, clinics, or for Health Management Organizations (HMOs), dispensing prescriptions, serving as a medical team consultant, or specializing in specific drug therapy areas, such as oncology or nuclear pharmacotherapy.

— EYE OPENERS —

Pharmacists are becoming more involved in making decisions regarding drug therapy and in counseling patients.

- Annual earnings (average): $89,820
- Annual earnings (starting): $64,350
- Employed: 230,000
- Growth: 24.6%
- Annual job openings: 16,000

PREPARING FOR THE JOB

Education/training required: First professional degree.

Programs: Clinical and industrial drug development (MS, PhD); clinical, hospital, and managed care pharmacy (MS, PhD); industrial and physical pharmacy and cosmetic sciences (MS, PhD); medicinal and pharmaceutical chemistry (MS, PhD); natural products chemistry and pharmacognosy (MS, PhD); pharmaceutics and drug design (MS, PhD); pharmaceutical economics (MS, PhD); pharmacy (PharmD [USA] PharmD, BS/BPharm [Canada]); pharmacy administration and pharmacy policy and regulatory affairs (MS, PhD).

Knowledge/courses: Medicine and dentistry; chemistry; therapy and counseling; biology; psychology; customer and personal service; mathematics; computers and electronics.

Licensure/certification: Licensure required.

WORKING CONDITIONS

Physical: Indoors; disease or infections; standing; repetitive motions.

Work settings: Community and hospital pharmacies.

Other job characteristics: Need to be exact or accurate; errors have important consequences; repeat same tasks.

— TOP SKILLS —

- Science
- Reading comprehension
- Social perceptiveness
- Active listening
- Instructing
- Mathematics

OTHER FACTS

O*NET code: 29-1051.00

GOE Information: Interest area: 08. Health Science. Work group: 08.02. Medicine and Surgery.

Personality type: Investigative. Investigative occupations frequently involve working with ideas and require an extensive amount of thinking. These occupations can involve searching for facts and figuring out problems.

WHERE TO FIND OUT MORE

For information on pharmacy as a career, contact

➤ American Association of Colleges of Pharmacy, 1426 Prince St., Alexandria, VA 22314. Internet: www.aacp.org

➤ American Pharmacists Association, 2215 Constitution Ave. NW, Washington, DC 20037-2985. Internet: www.aphanet.org

➤ National Association of Boards of Pharmacy, 1600 Feehanville Dr., Mount Prospect, IL 60056. Internet: www.nabp.net

First Professional Degree

QUICK LOOK

Diagnose and treat diseases and deformities of the human foot. Treat bone, muscle, and joint disorders affecting the feet. Diagnose diseases and deformities of the foot, using medical histories, physical examinations, X-rays, and laboratory test results. Prescribe medications, corrective devices, physical therapy, or surgery. Treat conditions such as corns, calluses, ingrown nails, tumors, shortened tendons, bunions, cysts, and abscesses by surgical methods. Advise patients about treatments and foot care techniques necessary for prevention of future problems. Refer patients to physicians when symptoms indicative of systemic disorders, such as arthritis or diabetes, are observed in feet and legs. Correct deformities by means of plaster casts and strapping. Make and fit prosthetic appliances. Perform administrative duties such as hiring employees, ordering supplies, and keeping records. Educate the public about the benefits of foot care through techniques such as speaking engagements, advertising, and other forums. Treat deformities by using mechanical methods, such as whirlpool or paraffin baths, and electrical methods, such as shortwave and low-voltage currents.

EYE OPENERS

Opportunities for newly trained podiatrists will be better in group medical practices, clinics, and health networks than in traditional, solo practices.

- Annual earnings (average): $100,550
- Annual earnings (starting): $43,990
- Employed: 10,000
- Growth: 16.2%
- Annual job openings: 1,000

PREPARING FOR THE JOB

Education/training required: First professional degree.

Programs: Podiatric medicine/podiatry (DPM).

Knowledge/courses: Medicine and dentistry; biology; therapy and counseling; sales and marketing; chemistry; customer and personal service; psychology; economics and accounting.

Licensure/certification: Licensure required; certification available for certain specializations.

WORKING CONDITIONS

Physical: Indoors; contaminants; disease or infections; sitting; using hands on objects, tools, or controls; repetitive motions.

Work settings: Private offices or clinics, group-practice offices, health-care organizations, hospitals, and other health-care facilities.

Other job characteristics: Need to be exact or accurate; errors have important consequences; repeat same tasks.

── TOP SKILLS ──

- Science
- Active listening
- Complex problem solving
- Management of financial resources
- Reading comprehension
- Active learning

OTHER FACTS

O*NET code: 29-1081.00

GOE information: Interest area: 08. Health Science. Work group: 08.04. Health Specialties.

Personality type: Social. Social occupations frequently involve working with, communicating with, and teaching people. These occupations often involve helping or providing service to others.

WHERE TO FIND OUT MORE

For information on a career in podiatric medicine, contact

➤ American Podiatric Medical Association, 9312 Old Georgetown Rd., Bethesda, MD 20814-1621. Internet: www.apma.org

Information on colleges of podiatric medicine and their entrance requirements, curricula, and student financial aid is available from

➤ American Association of Colleges of Podiatric Medicine, 15850 Crabbs Branch Way, Suite 320, Rockville, MD 20855-2622. Internet: www.aacpm.org

First Professional Degree

Psychiatrists

QUICK LOOK

Diagnose, treat, and help prevent disorders of the mind. Analyze and evaluate patient data and test findings to diagnose nature and extent of mental disorder. Prescribe, direct, and administer psychotherapeutic treatments or medications to treat mental, emotional, or behavioral disorders. Collaborate with physicians, psychologists, social workers, psychiatric nurses, or other professionals to discuss treatment plans and progress. Gather and maintain patient information and records, including social and medical history obtained from patients, relatives, and other professionals. Counsel outpatients and other patients during office visits. Design individualized care plans, using a variety of treatments. Examine or conduct laboratory or diagnostic tests on patient to provide information on general physical condition and mental disorder. Advise and inform guardians, relatives, and significant others of patients' conditions and treatment. Review and evaluate treatment procedures and outcomes of other psychiatrists and medical professionals. Teach, conduct research, and publish findings to increase understanding of mental, emotional, and behavioral states and disorders. Prepare and submit case reports and summaries to government and mental health agencies. Serve on committees to promote and maintain community mental health services and delivery systems.

— EYE OPENERS —

Unlike most other mental health professionals, psychiatrists can conduct physical examinations and order brain-imaging studies.

- Annual earnings (average): More than $145,600
- Annual earnings (starting): $63,820
- Employed: 567,000
- Growth: 24.0%
- Annual job openings: 41,000

Our sources did not provide separate job openings data for this occupation. The figures for employment and job openings listed here are shared with anesthesiologists, family and general practitioners, internists, obstetricians and gynecologists, pediatricians, and surgeons.

PREPARING FOR THE JOB

Education/training required: First professional degree.

Programs: Child psychiatry; physical, medical and rehabilitation psychiatry; psychiatry.

Knowledge/courses: Therapy and counseling; medicine and dentistry; psychology; biology; philosophy and theology; sociology and anthropology; chemistry; education and training.

Licensure/certification: Licensure required; certification available for certain specializations.

WORKING CONDITIONS

Physical: Indoors; disease or infections; sitting.

Work settings: Private offices or clinics, group-practice offices, health-care organizations, hospitals, and other health-care facilities.

Other job characteristics: Errors have important consequences; need to be exact or accurate.

OTHER FACTS

O*NET code: 29-1066.00

GOE information: Interest area: 08. Health Science. Work group: 08.02. Medicine and Surgery.

Personality type: Investigative. Investigative occupations frequently involve working with ideas and require an extensive amount of thinking. These occupations can involve searching for facts and figuring out problems.

TOP SKILLS

- Social perceptiveness
- Science
- Persuasion
- Systems analysis
- Active learning
- Active listening

WHERE TO FIND OUT MORE

For a list of medical schools and residency programs, as well as information on premedical education, financial aid, and medicine as a career, contact

➤ Association of American Medical Colleges, 2450 N St. NW, Washington, DC 20037-1126. Internet: www.aamc.org

➤ American Association of Colleges of Osteopathic Medicine, 5550 Friendship Blvd., Suite 310, Chevy Chase, MD 20815-7231. Internet: www.aacom.org

➤ American Medical Association, 515 N. State St., Chicago, IL 60610. Internet: www.ama-assn.org

➤ American Psychiatric Association, 1000 Wilson Blvd., Suite 1825, Arlington, VA 22209-3901. Internet: www.psych.org

First Professional Degree

QUICK LOOK

Treat diseases, injuries, and deformities by invasive methods, such as manual manipulation or by using instruments and appliances. Analyze patient's medical history, medication allergies, physical condition, and examination results to verify an operation's necessity and to determine best procedure. Operate on patients to correct deformities, repair injuries, prevent and treat diseases, or improve or restore patients' function. Follow established surgical techniques during the operation. Prescribe preoperative and postoperative treatments and procedures, such as sedatives, diets, antibiotics, and preparation and treatment of the patient's operative area. Examine patient to provide information on medical condition and surgical risk. Diagnose bodily disorders and orthopedic conditions and provide treatments, such as medicines and surgeries, in clinics, hospital wards, and operating rooms. Direct and coordinate activities of nurses, assistants, specialists, residents, and other medical staff. Provide consultation and surgical assistance to other physicians and surgeons. Refer patient to medical specialist or other practitioners when necessary. Examine instruments, equipment, and operating room to ensure sterility. Prepare case histories. Manage surgery services, including planning, scheduling and coordination, determination of procedures, and procurement of supplies and equipment. Conduct research to develop and test surgical techniques that can improve operating procedures and outcomes.

PREPARING FOR THE JOB

Education/training required: First professional degree.

Programs: Adult reconstructive orthopedics (orthopedic surgery); colon and rectal surgery; critical care surgery; general surgery; hand surgery; neurological surgery/neurosurgery; orthopedic surgery of the spine; orthopedics/orthopedic surgery; otolaryngology; pediatric orthopedics; pediatric surgery; plastic surgery; sports medicine; thoracic surgery; urology; vascular surgery.

Knowledge/courses: Medicine and dentistry; biology; therapy and counseling; psychology; chemistry; customer and personal service; personnel and human resources; economics and accounting.

Licensure/certification: Licensure required; certification available for certain specializations.

WORKING CONDITIONS

Physical: Indoors; contaminants; radiation; disease or infections; standing; using hands on objects, tools, or controls.

Work settings: Private offices and clinics, group-practice offices, health-care organizations, or hospitals and other health-care facilities.

Other job characteristics: Need to be exact or accurate; errors have important consequences; repeat same tasks.

TOP SKILLS

- Science
- Reading comprehension
- Judgment and decision making
- Management of financial resources
- Complex problem solving
- Critical thinking

OTHER FACTS

O*NET code: 29-1067.00

GOE information: Interest area: 08. Health Science. Work group: 08.02. Medicine and Surgery.

Personality type: Investigative. Investigative occupations frequently involve working with ideas and require an extensive amount of thinking. These occupations can involve searching for facts and figuring out problems.

WHERE TO FIND OUT MORE

For information on medical education and medicine as a career, contact

➤ Association of American Medical Colleges, 2450 N St. NW, Washington, DC 20037-1126. Internet: www.aamc.org

➤ American Association of Colleges of Osteopathic Medicine, 5550 Friendship Blvd., Suite 310, Chevy Chase, MD 20815-7231. Internet: www.aacom.org

➤ American College of Surgeons, Division of Education, 633 N. Saint Clair St., Chicago, IL 60611-3211. Internet: www.facs.org

First Professional Degree

QUICK LOOK

Diagnose and treat diseases and dysfunctions of animals. **May engage in a particular function, such as research and development, consultation, administration, technical writing, sale or production of commercial products, or rendering of technical services to commercial firms or other organizations.** Examine animals to detect and determine the nature of diseases or injuries. Treat sick or injured animals by prescribing medication, setting bones, dressing wounds, or performing surgery. Inoculate animals against various diseases, such as rabies and distemper. Collect body tissue, feces, blood, urine, or other body fluids for examination and analysis. Operate diagnostic equipment such as radiographic and ultrasound equipment and interpret the resulting images. Advise animal owners regarding sanitary measures, feeding, and general care necessary to promote health of animals. Educate the public about diseases that can be spread from animals to humans. Train and supervise workers who handle and care for animals. Provide care to a wide range of animals or specialize in a particular species, such as horses or exotic birds. Euthanize animals. Establish and conduct quarantine and testing procedures that prevent the spread of diseases to other animals or to humans and that comply with applicable government regulations. Conduct postmortem studies and analyses to determine the causes of animals' deaths. Perform administrative duties such as scheduling appointments, accepting payments from clients, and maintaining business records. Drive mobile clinic vans to farms so that health problems can be treated or prevented. Direct the overall operations of animal hospitals, clinics, or mobile services to farms. Specialize in a particular type of treatment such as dentistry, pathology, nutrition, surgery, microbiology, or internal medicine. Inspect and test horses, sheep, poultry, cattle, and other animals to detect the presence of communicable diseases. Research diseases to which animals could be susceptible. Plan and execute animal nutrition and reproduction programs. Inspect animal housing facilities to determine their cleanliness and adequacy. Determine the effects of drug therapies, antibiotics, or new surgical techniques by testing them on animals.

EYE OPENERS

Competition for admission to veterinary school is keen; however, graduates should have very good job opportunities.

- Annual earnings (average): $68,910
- Annual earnings (starting): $40,960
- Employed: 61,000
- Growth: 17.4%
- Annual job openings: 8,000

PREPARING FOR THE JOB

Education/training required: First professional degree.

Programs: Comparative and laboratory animal medicine; laboratory animal medicine; veterinary anatomy (Cert, MS, PhD); veterinary anesthesiology; veterinary dentistry; veterinary emergency and critical care medicine; veterinary internal medicine; veterinary medicine (DVM); veterinary nutrition; veterinary pathology; veterinary preventive medicine; veterinary radiology; veterinary surgery; veterinary toxicology; veterinary toxicology and pharmacology (Cert, MS, PhD); zoological medicine.

Knowledge/courses: Biology; medicine and dentistry; chemistry; therapy and counseling; sales and marketing; customer and personal service; psychology; education and training.

Licensure/certification: Licensure required.

WORKING CONDITIONS

Physical: Indoors; noisy; contaminants; disease or infections; standing; using hands on objects, tools, or controls.

Work settings: Offices, kennels, farms, laboratories, or meat-processing plants.

Other job characteristics: Need to be exact or accurate; errors have important consequences; repeat same tasks.

TOP SKILLS

- Science
- Management of financial resources
- Reading comprehension
- Judgment and decision making
- Complex problem solving
- Management of personnel resources

OTHER FACTS

O*NET code: 29-1131.00

GOE Information: Interest area: 08. Health Science. Work group: 08.05. Animal Care.

Personality type: Investigative. Investigative occupations frequently involve working with ideas and require an extensive amount of thinking. These occupations can involve searching for facts and figuring out problems.

WHERE TO FIND OUT MORE

For additional information on careers in veterinary medicine, contact

➤ American Veterinary Medical Association, 1931 N. Meacham Rd., Suite 100, Schaumburg, IL 60173-4360. Internet: www.avma.org

➤ Association of American Veterinary Medical Colleges, 1101 Vermont Ave. NW, Suite 301, Washington, DC 20005. Internet: www.aavmc.org

First Professional Degree

Technical Help in Using the DVD

System Requirements

To view the DVD and hear its narration, you need a PC/Mac with a DVD drive, DVD player software (such as Windows Media Player), and speakers.

Steps for Viewing the DVD

1. Insert the DVD into the DVD drive.

Note: Be sure that the drive runs DVDs and is not just a CD drive.

2. After a few moments, the DVD player software installed on your computer should start automatically and show you the Health-Care CareerVision DVD menu.

Note: If the player does not run automatically, start the player and then play/run the DVD. If you need assistance in running the DVD, use your player's Help menu.

3. Click the "Next Page" and "Previous Page" arrows at the bottom of the screen to navigate the DVD menu.

4. From the DVD menu, click the number or job title of the video you wish to view.

Note: If you do not hear the video narration, confirm that the computer has speakers and that the volume is not muted. Turn up the volume as needed.

Other Information to Note

DVD Viewable Through Television DVD Players. The DVD is also viewable from your television DVD player. However, because the DVD was designed for computer viewing, the DVD menus may lack some resolution.

Videos Appearing Twice on the DVD. Radiologic Technicians and Radiologic Technologists are described in one video. Therefore, the video appears twice as video 37 and video 38 on the DVD for your convenience. Clinical Psychologists and Counseling Psychologists are described in one video. Therefore, the video appears twice as video 61 and video 62 on the DVD for your convenience.

The Book Contains the Most Current Information. You may occasionally notice statements in the videos that are not consistent with the written information in the book. This can happen because the book uses the latest information.

In particular, statements in the book about requirements for education, training, and licensure are based on the most current edition of the *Occupational Outlook Handbook* by the U.S. Department of Labor. Because requirements often vary in different jurisdictions, be sure to investigate the requirements where you live or intend to work.

Background on the Career Information Used in This Book

The information we used in creating this book came mostly from databases created by the U.S. Department of Labor and the U.S. Census Bureau. Most of the facts about jobs are derived from the Department of Labor's O*NET (Occupational Information Network) database, which is now the primary source of detailed information on occupations. The Labor Department updates the O*NET on a regular basis, and we used the most recent one available—O*NET release 11.

Information in a database format can be boring and even confusing, so we did many things to help make the printed data useful and present it to you in a form that is easy to understand. To get the information on education or training required for the job, we used a crosswalk created by the National Crosswalk Service Center to connect information in the Classification of Instructional Programs (CIP) to O*NET job titles. We made various changes to connect the O*NET job titles to the education or training programs related to them and also modified the names of some education and training programs so they would be more easily understood.

Because we wanted to include information about earnings, growth, number of openings, and other data not in the O*NET, we cross-referenced information developed by the U.S. Bureau of Labor Statistics (BLS) and the U.S. Census Bureau. This information is the most reliable data we could obtain. For data on these topics, the BLS uses a slightly different set of job titles than the O*NET uses, so we had to match similar titles. By linking the BLS and U.S. Census data to the O*NET job titles in this book, we tied information about growth, earnings, and characteristics of workers to all the job titles in this book.

Other sources of information include the following:

➤ The information about licensing and certification, work settings, and organizations related to each job is derived from the *Occupational Outlook Handbook (OOH),* which is updated biennially by the U.S. Department of Labor and published by JIST.

➤ The overview of the health-care field in Chapter 1 is based on the *Career Guide to Industries,* which is published by the U.S. Department of Labor on the same update cycle as the *OOH*. The statistics are based on 2004 figures because these are the most recent available.

➤ The career videos on the DVD were developed and distributed by the New Jersey Center for Occupational Employment Information under a grant from the U.S. Department of Labor, Employment and Training Administration. They are designed to provide a brief, visual introduction to careers and the world of work.

Facts About the Eye Openers

The Eye Openers boxes in the Chapter 4 job descriptions include information on earnings, projected growth, and number of job openings for each occupation. This section explains the complexities inherent in the sources of this information and what we did to make sense of them.

The employment security agency of each state gathers information on earnings for various jobs and forwards it to the U.S. Bureau of Labor Statistics. This information is organized in standardized ways by a BLS program called Occupational Employment Statistics (OES). To keep the earnings for the various jobs and regions comparable, the OES screens out certain types of earnings and includes others, so the OES earnings we use in this book represent straight-time gross pay exclusive of premium pay. More specifically, the OES earnings include the job's base rate; cost-of-living allowances; guaranteed pay; hazardous-duty pay; incentive pay, including commissions and production bonuses; on-call pay; and tips, but they do not include back pay, jury duty pay, overtime pay, severance pay, shift differentials, nonproduction bonuses, or tuition reimbursements. Also, self-employed workers are not included in the estimates, and they can be a significant segment of workers in certain occupations.

For average earnings, we use the median figure—half of workers earn more, half less. For starting earnings, we use the figure for the 10th percentile; in other words, 10 percent of workers earn less than this amount.

The information on projected growth and number of job openings comes from the Office of Occupational Statistics and Employment Projections, a program within the Bureau of Labor Statistics that develops information about projected trends in the nation's labor market for the next 10 years. The most recent projections available cover the years from 2004 to 2014. The projections are based on information about people moving into and out of occupations. The BLS uses data from various sources in projecting the growth and number of openings for each job title. Some data comes from the Census Bureau's Current Population Survey, and some comes from an OES survey. The projections assume that there will be no major economic upheaval.

Perhaps you're wondering why we present figures on both job growth *and* number of openings. Aren't these two ways of saying the same thing? Actually, you need to know both.

Consider the occupation occupational therapist assistants, which is projected to grow at the astounding rate of 34.1 percent. There should be lots of opportunities in such a fast-growing job, right? Not exactly. This is a very small occupation, with only about 21,000 people currently employed, so even though it is growing rapidly, it is expected to create only 2,000 job openings per year. Now consider medical secretaries. This occupation is growing at the rate of 17.0 percent, which is only a little better than the average for all occupations. Nevertheless, this is a large occupation that employs almost 400,000 workers, so even though its growth rate is not special, this occupation is expected to take on 55,000 new workers each year. That's why we base our selection of the best jobs on both of these economic indicators and why you should pay attention to both when you scan the lists of best jobs in Chapter 3.

The Limits of the Data in This Book

In this book we use the most reliable and up-to-date information available on earnings, projected growth, number of openings, and other topics. The earnings data came from the U.S. Department of Labor's Bureau of Labor Statistics. As you look at the figures, keep in mind that they are estimates. They give you a general idea about the number of workers employed, annual earnings, rate of job growth, and annual job openings.

Understand that a problem with such data is that it describes an average. Just as there is no precisely average person, there is no such thing as a statistically average example of a particular job. We say this because data, although helpful, can also be misleading.

Take, for example, the average yearly earnings information in this book. The Bureau of Labor Statistics obtains this highly reliable data from a very large U.S. working population sample. It tells us the average annual pay received in May 2005 by people in various job titles (actually, it is the median annual pay, which means that half earned more and half less).

When you look at the average earnings number, it's important to remember that half of all people in that occupation earn less than that amount. For example, people who are new to the occupation or with only a few years of work experience often earn much less than the median amount. People who live in rural areas or who work for smaller employers typically earn less than those who do similar work in cities (where the cost of living is higher) or for bigger employers. People in certain areas of the country earn less than those in others. Other factors also influence how much you are likely to earn in a given job in your area.

For example, dentists in the New York metropolitan area earn an average of $124,540 per year, whereas dentists in six metropolitan areas in North Carolina earn an average of over $145,600 per year. Although the cost of living tends to be higher in the New York area, North Carolina has only one dentistry school, and therefore dentists there experience less competition for patients and can command higher fees. So you can see that many factors can cause earnings to vary widely.

Also keep in mind that the figures for job growth and number of openings are projections by labor economists—their best guesses about what we can expect between now and 2014. They are not guarantees. A major economic downturn or technological breakthrough could change the actual outcome.

Finally, don't forget that the job market consists of both job openings and job seekers. The figures on job growth and openings don't tell you how many people will be competing with you to be hired. The Department of Labor does not publish figures on the supply of job candidates, so we are unable to tell you about the level of competition you can expect. Competition is an important issue that you should research for any tentative career goal. In some cases, the *Occupational Outlook Handbook* provides informative statements. You should speak to people who educate or train tomorrow's workers; they probably have a good idea of how many of their graduates find rewarding employment and how quickly. People in the workforce also can provide insights into this issue. Use your critical thinking skills to evaluate what people tell you. For example, recruiters for training programs are highly motivated to get you to sign up, whereas people in the workforce may be trying to discourage you from competing. Get a variety of opinions to balance out possible biases.

So, in reviewing the information in this book, please understand the limitations of the data. As in most other things in life, you need to use common sense when making career decisions.

Definitions of Top Skills

Here are the definitions of the top skills listed with the job descriptions in Chapter 4. These definitions help you more fully understand the specific skills needed for a particular health-care career.

Skill Name	Definition
Active learning	Understanding the implications of new information for both current and future problem solving and decision making
Active listening	Giving full attention to what other people are saying, taking time to understand the points being made, asking questions as appropriate, and not interrupting at inappropriate times
Complex problem solving	Identifying difficult problems and reviewing related information in order to develop and evaluate options and implement solutions
Coordination	Adjusting actions in relation to others' actions
Critical thinking	Using logic and reasoning to identify the strengths and weaknesses of alternative solutions, conclusions, or approaches to problems
Equipment maintenance	Performing routine maintenance on equipment and determining when and what kind of maintenance is needed
Equipment selection	Determining the kind of tools and equipment needed to do a job
Installation	Installing equipment, machines, wiring, or programs to meet specifications
Instructing	Teaching others how to do something

(continued)

Skill Name	Definition
Judgment and decision making	Considering the relative costs and benefits of potential actions in order to choose the most appropriate one
Learning strategies	Selecting and using training/instructional methods and procedures appropriate for the situation when learning or teaching new things
Management of financial resources	Determining how money will be spent to complete work and accounting for these expenditures
Management of material resources	Obtaining and seeing to the appropriate use of equipment, facilities, and materials needed to do certain work
Management of personnel resources	Motivating, developing, and directing people as they work and identifying the best people for the job
Mathematics	Using mathematics to solve problems
Monitoring	Assessing your performance or that of other individuals or organizations in order to make improvements or take corrective action
Negotiation	Bringing others together and trying to reconcile differences
Operation and control	Controlling operations of equipment or systems
Operation monitoring	Watching gauges, dials, or other indicators to make sure a machine is working properly
Operations analysis	Analyzing needs and product requirements to create a design
Persuasion	Convincing others to change their minds or behavior
Programming	Writing computer programs for various purposes
Quality control analysis	Conducting tests and inspections of products, services, or processes in order to evaluate quality or performance
Reading comprehension	Understanding written sentences and paragraphs in work-related documents
Repairing	Fixing machines or systems by using the needed tools

Skill Name	Definition
Science	Using scientific rules and methods to solve problems
Service orientation	Actively looking for ways to help people
Social perceptiveness	Being aware of others' reactions and understanding why they react as they do
Speaking	Talking to others in order to convey information effectively
Systems analysis	Determining how a system should work and how changes in conditions, operations, and the environment will affect outcomes
Systems evaluation	Identifying measures or indicators of system performance and the actions needed to improve or correct performance relative to the goals of the system
Technology design	Generating or adapting equipment and technology to serve user needs
Time management	Managing one's own time and the time of others
Troubleshooting	Determining causes of operating errors and deciding what to do about them
Writing	Communicating effectively in writing as appropriate for the needs of the audience

Understanding the GOE System That Organizes Jobs by Interests

Chapter 4 lists the interest areas and work groups for each job described under "GOE information." The GOE is the Guide for Occupational Exploration, a system for exploring jobs based on your interests. In the *New Guide for Occupational Exploration* published by JIST, occupations are organized into 16 interest areas based on the U.S. Department of Education career clusters.

We thought you would want to see the complete GOE organizational system so you would understand how any job that interests you fits into this structure. Although most of the jobs in this book are assigned to the interest area "08 Health Science," several are assigned to other areas. For example, emergency medical technicians and paramedics belong in "12 Law and Public Safety," and fitness trainers and aerobics instructors belong in "05 Education and Training."

Interest areas have two-digit code numbers; the more-specific work groups have four-digit code numbers beginning with the code number for the interest area in which they are classified. These are the 16 GOE interest areas and work groups:

01 Agriculture and Natural Resources

      01.01 Managerial Work in Agriculture and Natural Resources

      01.02 Resource Science/Engineering for Plants, Animals, and the Environment

      01.03 Resource Technologies for Plants, Animals, and the Environment

      01.04 General Farming

      01.05 Nursery, Groundskeeping, and Pest Control

01.06 Forestry and Logging

01.07 Hunting and Fishing

01.08 Mining and Drilling

02 Architecture and Construction

02.01 Managerial Work in Architecture and Construction

02.02 Architectural Design

02.03 Architecture/Construction Engineering Technologies

02.04 Construction Crafts

02.05 Systems and Equipment Installation, Maintenance, and Repair

02.06 Construction Support/Labor

03 Arts and Communication

03.01 Managerial Work in Arts and Communication

03.02 Writing and Editing

03.03 News, Broadcasting, and Public Relations

03.04 Studio Art

03.05 Design

03.06 Drama

03.07 Music

03.08 Dance

03.09 Media Technology

03.10 Communications Technology

03.11 Musical Instrument Repair

04 Business and Administration

04.01 Managerial Work in General Business

04.02 Managerial Work in Business Detail

04.03 Human Resources Support

04.04 Secretarial Support

04.05 Accounting, Auditing, and Analytical Support

04.06 Mathematical Clerical Support

04.07 Records and Materials Processing

04.08 Clerical Machine Operation

05 Education and Training

05.01 Managerial Work in Education

05.02 Preschool, Elementary, and Secondary Teaching and Instructing

05.03 Postsecondary and Adult Teaching and Instructing

05.04 Library Services

05.05 Archival and Museum Services

05.06 Counseling, Health, and Fitness Education

06 Finance and Insurance

06.01 Managerial Work in Finance and Insurance

06.02 Finance/Insurance Investigation and Analysis

06.03 Finance/Insurance Records Processing

06.04 Finance/Insurance Customer Service

06.05 Finance/Insurance Sales and Support

07 Government and Public Administration

07.01 Managerial Work in Government and Public Administration

07.02 Public Planning

07.03 Regulations Enforcement

07.04 Public Administration Clerical Support

08 Health Science

08.01 Managerial Work in Medical and Health Services

08.02 Medicine and Surgery

08.03 Dentistry

08.04 Health Specialties

08.05 Animal Care

08.06 Medical Technology

08.07 Medical Therapy

08.08 Patient Care and Assistance

08.09 Health Protection and Promotion

09 Hospitality, Tourism, and Recreation

09.01 Managerial Work in Hospitality and Tourism

09.02 Recreational Services

09.03 Hospitality and Travel Services

09.04 Food and Beverage Preparation

09.05 Food and Beverage Service

09.06 Sports

09.07 Barber and Beauty Services

10 Human Service

10.01 Counseling and Social Work

10.02 Religious Work

10.03 Child/Personal Care and Services

10.04 Client Interviewing

11 Information Technology

11.01 Managerial Work in Information Technology

11.02 Information Technology Specialties

11.03 Digital Equipment Repair

12 Law and Public Safety

12.01 Managerial Work in Law and Public Safety

12.02 Legal Practice and Justice Administration

12.03 Legal Support

12.04 Law Enforcement and Public Safety

12.05 Safety and Security

12.06 Emergency Responding

12.07 Military

13 Manufacturing

13.01 Managerial Work in Manufacturing

13.02 Machine Setup and Operation

13.03 Production Work, Assorted Materials Processing

13.04 Welding, Brazing, and Soldering

13.05 Production Machining Technology

13.06 Production Precision Work

13.07 Production Quality Control

13.08 Graphic Arts Production

13.09 Hands-On Work, Assorted Materials

13.10 Woodworking Technology

13.11 Apparel, Shoes, Leather, and Fabric Care

13.12 Electrical and Electronic Repair

13.13 Machinery Repair

13.14 Vehicle and Facility Mechanical Work

13.15 Medical and Technical Equipment Repair

13.16 Utility Operation and Energy Distribution

13.17 Loading, Moving, Hoisting, and Conveying

14 Retail and Wholesale Sales and Service

14.01 Managerial Work in Retail/Wholesale Sales and Service

14.02 Technical Sales

14.03 General Sales

14.04 Personal Soliciting

14.05 Purchasing

14.06 Customer Service

Resources for Further Exploration

The facts and pointers in this book provide a good overview of health-care jobs. If you want additional details on careers, education, and job searching, we suggest you consult the resources listed here. All of the books are published by JIST; visit www.jist.com for more details.

Books on Careers and Career Planning

For more facts about careers, take a look at the following books:

➤ *Top 100 Health-Care Careers:* This guide by Dr. Saul Wischnitzer and Edith Wischnitzer offers detailed information on health-care careers. It overviews 100 jobs and explains required education and training, lists education programs, discusses health-care education admissions tests, explains how to relate to patients, shows how to prepare for your job search, and much more.

➤ *Occupational Outlook Handbook:* Updated every two years by the U.S. Department of Labor, this book provides descriptions for almost 270 major jobs covering more than 85 percent of the workforce. For a quick-reading version of the *OOH,* consult the *EZ Occupational Outlook Handbook* from JIST.

➤ *Enhanced Occupational Outlook Handbook:* Includes all descriptions in the *OOH* plus descriptions of more than 6,300 more-specialized jobs related to them.

➤ *O*NET Dictionary of Occupational Titles:* This book is the only printed source of the more than 900 jobs described in the U.S. Department of Labor's Occupational Information Network database. It covers all the jobs in the book you're now reading, but it offers more topics than we were able to fit here.

➤ *New Guide for Occupational Exploration:* This important career reference allows you to explore all major O*NET jobs based on your interests.

➤ *50 Best Jobs for Your Personality:* Explore the best career fit for your personality type through interesting "best jobs" lists and detailed job descriptions. Part of JIST's best-selling Best Jobs series.

➤ *Overnight Career Choice:* For information on career decision making and planning, read this book by Michael Farr. It can help you choose a career goal based on a variety of criteria, including skills, interests, and values. It is part of the Help in a Hurry series, so it is designed to produce quick results.

Books on College Majors

➤ *College Majors Handbook with Real Career Paths and Payoffs:* The only book that provides information on the actual jobs and earnings of college graduates in 60 majors. Based on a U.S. Census Bureau study of 150,000 college graduates, this handbook offers accurate and helpful information for making decisions on a college major. Authors Neeta Fogg, Paul Harrington, and Thomas Harrington explain which majors are the best investment, the job and salary prospects for specific majors, and how many of a major's graduates go on to additional education.

➤ *90-Minute College Major Matcher:* This book leads you through a fast and easy method of connecting yourself to a major and a career. Checklists reveal your interests (personality type), skills, and favorite courses. With Laurence Shatkin's guidance, you use this information to match yourself to the best major and occupation.

Resources on Job Hunting

If you are looking for a job, check out the following resources:

➤ *Expert Resumes for Health Care Careers:* This collection of resumes is aimed at people seeking health-care jobs at all levels—from allied health technicians to physicians. In addition to hundreds of pages of sample resumes, Wendy Enelow and Louise Kursmark present sound resume-writing advice, including how to create and use an electronic resume and whether to use a resume or a CV.

➤ *The Ultimate Job Search:* Million-selling career author and consultant Richard H. Beatty shares the inside scoop on self-assessment and job objectives, powerful resumes and cover letters, working with search firms and employment agencies, want ads, the Internet, direct-mail job search campaigns, networking, interviewing, negotiating job offers, and succeeding on the new job.

➤ **Job Banks by Occupation:** This set of links is offered by America's Career InfoNet. At www.acinet.org, find the Career Tools box, click Career Resource Library, and then click Job & Resume Banks. The Job Banks by Occupation link leads you to groups of jobs such as "Healthcare Practitioners and Technical Occupations," which in turn lead you to more-specific job titles and occupation-specific job-listing sites maintained by various organizations.

➤ *Interview Magic:* Author Susan Britton Whitcomb reveals her inside secrets for excelling in job interviews and getting job offers. She clearly explains the nuts and bolts of interviewing and then illustrates the techniques with before-and-after interview responses. Worksheets coach you through the interview preparation process.

➤ *Next-Day Salary Negotiation:* Prepare tonight to get your best pay tomorrow. Author Maryanne Wegerbauer and the Editors at JIST give you negotiating help in a hurry. This book explains what to say in a negotiation and provides salary data for more than 250 top jobs. For a more comprehensive directory of salary information, consult the authoritative *Salary Facts Handbook* by the Editors at JIST.

INDEX

N

O

P

U

V

W–Z

Helping people help themselves in career and life.

Visit **www.jist.com**, our convenient Web site, to access information about JIST and our products. At **www.jist.com** you will find lots of FREE stuff and more:

- **Online Product Catalog**—Search, browse, and purchase materials online.
- **JIST's Quick Online Order Form**—Catalog handy? Use our quick order form. Simply enter the order codes and go!
- **Additional product information**—View tables of contents and sample pages from more than 80 JIST-published books.
- **Secure ordering**—We've made ordering online easy to use and secure.

- **JIST Online Assessment**—Administer several popular JIST career assessments online and get results delivered quickly to your desktop!
- **Monthly specials**—On selected JIST books, workbooks, videos, career assessments, and CD-ROMs!
- **Close-out bargains**—While supplies last!

Visit us often and take advantage of the best career and job search information available.

www.jist.com